365 DAYS OF CREATIVE PLAY

For Children 2 Yrs. & Up

3rd Edition

Sheila Ellison & Judith Gray

Sourcebook
Naperville, IL

Published by: **Sourcebooks, Inc.**
P.O. Box 372, Naperville, Illinois, 60566
(630) 961-3900
FAX: (630) 961-2168

Editorial: Todd Stocke
Cover Design: Wayne Johnson
Interior Design: Wayne Johnson, Sourcebooks, Inc.

Ellison, Sheila.
　　365 days of creative play : for children two years and up / by Sheila Ellison and Judith Gray. — 3rd ed.
　　　　p.　cm.
　　Includes index.
　　ISBN 1-57071-029-5 (pbk.) : $12.95
　　　　1. Creative activities and seat work. 2. Amusements. I. Gray, Judith Anne, date. II. Title. III. Three hundred sixty-five days of creative play.
　　GV1203.E363　1995
　　790.1'922—dc20
95-3261
CIP

Printed and bound in the United States of America
10　9

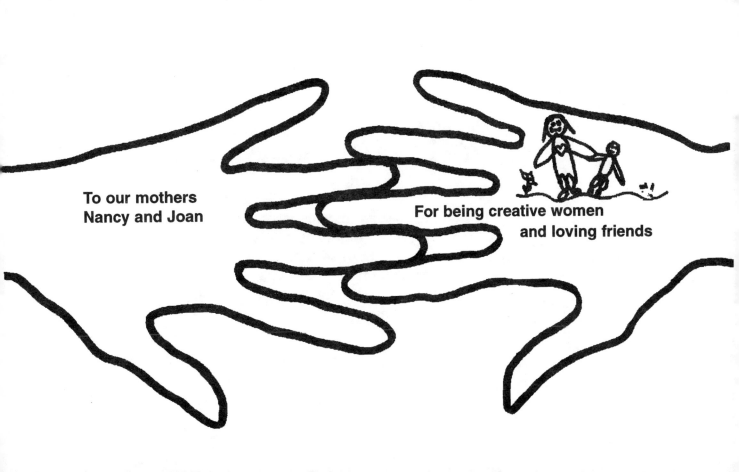

To our mothers
Nancy and Joan

For being creative women
and loving friends

Acknowledgement

The authors wish to thank Chris Calwell from the Natural Resources Defense Council (NRDC) for his assistance in ensuring the environmental soundness of the activities in this revised edition. One of NRDC's fastest growing projects is "Mothers and Others" for a livable planet. Its purpose is to empower families to protect the health of children through local and national environmental resources. The Mothers and Others newsletter, "tlc" (truly loving care) is full of practical, easy-to-read tips for families to make their home, school, and play environment safe and healthy.

For more information, please write to: Mothers and Others
                                         40 West 20th Street
                                         New York, NY 10011

Introduction

What your child becomes in life depends upon the experiences he or she has in the early years. Play provides the child with positive experiences and feelings of success and accomplishment. Creative play opportunities are critical in that they allow for imagination, growth, and problem-solving development. This book has been carefully designed to present a wide variety of creative projects for young children. It is to be read and used by adults—parents, teachers, and childcare providers—who serve as the child's motivators, facilitators, and co-participants.

There are 13 categories of activities, all of which tap into the child's creative potential. They are: Art, Construction, Craft, Dance, Education, Environment, Family, Foods and Cooking, Games, Horticulture, Make-Believe, Music, and Nature. If the activities are done in order, there is a sequential balance of categories. However, adults should not feel compelled to keep in chronological step and are encouraged to select suitable activities from the wealth of ideas anywhere in the book.

All the creative play activities have been tried and tested by the authors, who would appreciate suggestions and comments from parents, teachers, and other readers. New ideas will be gratefully included in the next edition. In addition, the authors have been careful to ensure that all the activities and their materials comply with safe environmental standards. Read and enjoy!

For Your Child's Safety and Enjoyment

✓ Spread newspaper over and beneath working surface

✓ Keep dangerous supplies out of reach or <u>closely</u> supervised

✓ Dress your child appropriately for the activities—loose and old clothes are best

✓ Carefully monitor the use of sharp tools and materials, such as scissors

✓ Check outdoor areas for sharp objects before starting outside activities

✓ Educate your child to recognize and avoid danger and harm

✓ Clean your child's hands before cooking activities

✓ Thoroughly wash and rinse brushes after use

✓ Do not force your child to do the activities

✓ Play *with* your child

✓ Read carefully through the **Materials** and **Directions** before each activity

✓ Adjust your time schedule—some activities take a few days, others a few minutes

✓ The finished product or experience is less important than the process itself

✓ Take this book with you while visiting or on vacation with your child

✓ Allow your child to use his or her own creativity—they may see things differently

✓ Keep this book handy at all times

✓ Other family members and friends may enjoy facilitating the activities

✓ Above all, establish a non-threatening, enjoyable play environment for all

Materials and Supplies

Art, Crafts, and Construction:

Crayons
Water-based pens or markers
Tempera paints
Paint brushes
Construction paper
Pipe cleaners
String or twine
Paper cups and plates
Fabric and felt remnants
Ribbons and bows
Old magazines
Tissue paper
Newspaper
Thread spools
Corks and bottle caps
Glue or paste

Paper bags
Used boxes
Colored pencils
Colored chalk
Egg cartons
Watercolor paints
Yarn
Adhesive tape
Plaster of paris
Old shirts
Aluminum foil
Butcher paper
Scissors
Masking tape
Straws
Toothpicks

Foods and Cooking:

Vegetable food coloring
Assorted bowls
Cereals
Dried fruits
Grains
Pudding mixes

Plastic wrap
Cookie cutters
Baking pans
Rolling Pin
Saucepans
Cookie sheet

Music, Games, and Make-Believe:

Bed sheets
Sequins
Family photos
Dress-up clothes
Tapes and records
Cardboard cartons and boxes
Balls
Playing cards
Milk and oatmeal cartons

Nature and Horticulture:

Potting soil
Pots—used clay or plastic
Seeds
Glass jars
Popsicle sticks
Small handheld gardening tools
Fresh vegetables
Spring bulbs
Unbleached coffee filters

Start here

Yarn Dog

Materials
1. Colored rug yarn or thick 8-ply knitting wool
2. Paper
3. White glue
4. Dog photos or pictures
5. Cardboard

Directions

Trace a good, clear picture of a dog, the larger the better, onto the cardboard. Cut the yarn or wool into 1" or 2" strands. Use an egg carton to separate the colors and to make selecting and handling of yarn easier. The child then glues the yarn strands onto the dog outline to make hair and a tail. Draw a mouth and eyes and define the ears and the tail. Finally, invent an appropriate name for the new dog.

2

DAD

Bedtime Ritual

Directions

Bedtime is a very important time for your child. Create a bedtime ritual which you repeat every night. This will give your child a sense of security and also something set to look forward to. Begin the ritual about an hour beforehand. Here is an example: Bath for 20 minutes with at least half that time for playing, read stories for another 20 minutes, spend 15 minutes together talking about all the good things that happened that day, and then take 5 minutes for a prayer or meditation which can be sung or spoken softly.

Mashed Potato Sculptures

Materials

1. Instant mashed potatoes
2. 2 eggs
3. Baking dish
4. Pastry brush
5. Modeling tools

Directions

Prepare the instant potatoes according to the package directions. Beat in 2 egg yolks. Empty mixture into the buttered baking dish. Using modeling tools such as toothpicks, teaspoons, forks, and popsicle sticks, form the potatoes into shapes—animals, faces, robots, etc. Beat the egg whites slightly and spread it onto the sculptures with the pastry brush. Bake in the oven at 350°F until brown and shiny. Cool slightly before serving.

Walking Collector

Materials
1. Bottle of glue with brush attached
2. Strong cardboard

Directions
Go for a walk with your child with the glue and cardboard in hand. As your child finds things, glue them onto the cardboard. Let her or him decide where the things should go and what to do with those things that won't stick.

Fabric Garden

5

Materials

1. Scraps of plain and floral fabric
2. Colored markers
3. Plain paper
4. White glue
5. Poster board

Directions

First cut out the flowers, leaves, stems, and buds from floral fabric. Plain fabric can be used to cut out additional petals, leaves, and stems. Use colored markers to outline the shapes. Glue all the shapes onto the paper to make them firmer. Let the glue dry completely. Reassemble the shapes on the poster board to make flowers, plants, and imaginary flora so that the finished effect is like a flower garden or field of flowers designed by your child.

 **6**

Sand Touching

Materials
1. Sandbox or beach

Directions
Your child digs his or her hands under the sand. When they are totally covered, suggest that they try to touch fingers. This is harder than it sounds. Also suggest that they shake hands. Next an adult or another child can bury their feet too and then try to touch toes while they are all under the sand. If the sand is damp, tunnels can be excavated from each end until hands and fingers meet.

By Bus, Boat or Train

7

Directions
Depending where you are living, it is possible to select a method of transportation that you and your child don't use often. If you drive everywhere in the car, for instance, then you might choose the local bus service for this activity. When you have a few hours to spare, take your child on a bus ride or a subway ride or a ferry ride. Simply purchase a round-trip ticket and enjoy the trip. This will undoubtedly prove educational for the both of you.

Pavement Painting

Materials
1. Plastic bucket
2. Large paint brushes
3. Old sponges
4. Water

Directions
On a dry, warm day give your child a plastic bucket of water, one or two paint brushes and an old sponge. Find a safe driveway, wooden deck, or pavement and let him or her paint large pictures or patterns with the water, right onto the cement or wood. Pictures will dry and disappear, but there will always be more room to paint as long as there is water in the bucket.

8

Spray Drums

9

Materials

1. Garden hose
2. Spray attachment (for hose)
3. Metal pots, pans, lids, bowls, etc.
4. Grassy space or level driveway

Directions

Turn the pots and pans upside down on the grass or driveway. Lean some of the larger lids or pans against a wall, bench, or tree. Attach the sprayer to the hose and turn on the water. Have the child spray the metal objects with water to make drumming sounds and rhythms. Experiment with varying intensities of water force—from dripping to torrential. Take frequent breaks to rearrange pots, pans, and lids. This activity should never be done during droughts.

My Tree and I

Materials
1. Tree seedling
2. Measuring tape
3. Camera and film
4. Scrapbook

Directions

Go to the plant nursery and buy a small, fast-growing tree —preferably have your child choose it. Plant the seedling in a special place in your garden. Take a photo of your child standing next to the tree. Measure the height of both the tree and your child and enter these measurements together with the date and the printed photo into the scrapbook. Every year, on the tree's birthday, take another photo and more measurements. Continue entering the details into the scrapbook. Compare growth rates and changes.

Ghost Land

Materials

1. Open space which is free of dangerous objects
2. Old sheet

Directions

11

Explain to your child that she or he is going to pretend to be a ghost and that she or he will be playing in ghost land. Cover your child with an old sheet and lead her or him into the middle of the space. Now watch the creative ideas and movements evolve from your child's imagination.

Poem Dance

Directions

Choose a favorite poem and read it aloud. Select a few of the ideas or images in the poem and express them in movement with your child. Some ideas will suggest how to move and others will suggest a mood, feeling, or environment. Some poems can be read and moved to for their rhythmic quality. In every case, dance with your child and make the poem come alive and be more meaningful.

12

Homemade Playdough

13

Materials
1. 1 cup of salt
2. 1 cup of flour
3. 1 cup of water
4. Cookie cutters
5. Rolling pin or narrow bottle
6. Food coloring (optional)

Directions
Put salt and flour in a deep unbreakable bowl.
Drape your child in an old shirt or smock and allow him or her to mix the dry ingredients thoroughly with hands or a wooden spoon. Slowly add water to which some drops of food coloring have been added. Continue to mix, then knead dough until it is smooth and elastic without being sticky. Dump the dough onto a flat floured surface and roll it out with the rolling pin or bottle. Use cookie cutters to make shapes or provide child with other cutting and poking utensils such as plastic knives, bottle tops and lids, chopsticks, and assorted plastic shapes.

14

Lighter Thoughts

Directions

Lie down by your child and both of you close your eyes. Talk softly to your child. Say that you are both lying in the shade and that it is warm and quiet. Take deep breaths and imagine you are breathing in the warmth and the silence. Breathe out the sad and uncomfortable thoughts. Continue to breathe in happy, light thoughts and breathe out the unpleasant ones until you are filled with love and happiness. You and your child will feel closer to your own selves and to each other.

Homemade Butter Balls

Materials
1. Whipping cream
2. Empty baby food jar
3. Crackers

15

Directions

Pour one tablespoon of cream into a baby food jar. Screw on the lid and shake vigorously. Soon a lump of solid butter will form inside the jar. Remove the butter ball and spread on some crackers. Add flavorings or colors if you like.

Sand Saucers

Materials
1. Sand or fine dirt
2. Old saucers or foil plates
3. Flowers, leaves, seeds
4. Buttons, shells, feathers, and other small objects

Directions
Fill saucer or plate with damp sand and mound slightly. Press the flowers, etc., and other small objects into the sand making designs, scenes, or mandalas. Sand saucers last a couple of days if sand is kept moist, and they make nice table decorations.

16

Penny Can

Materials
1. Plastic or metal cylinder with a plastic fitting lid, e.g., nuts can
2. Assorted stickers, stamps, and gummed labels
3. Masking tape
4. Colored markers

Directions

Completely cover the outside of the cylinder with stickers, stamps, and labels. Use white glue to attach if necessary. Make a small slit in the plastic lid big enough for a penny to go through. Put the lid on and tape it down securely. Use colored markers to decorate or conceal the tape. There will be more incentive to save pennies when the "bank" has been self-constructed.

18

Animal Sounds

Directions

This is a guessing game. Take turns with your child to guess what the animal is from the sound that is being made. For example, you make the sound of an elephant and your child tries to guess the animal from the sound it makes. Encourage your child to be as creative and animated as possible.

I See

Materials

1. Illustrated magazines

19

Directions

Sit with your child and turn the pages of the magazine. Ask your child what he or she likes to see. Then ask your child why. And ask what is his or her favorite thing to watch. Discuss the sense of sight with your child and how it has been developed in us so that we can find out about our environment and ourselves. Sight is for looking and learning. This activity can also be done while taking a walk with your child. Also, it is interesting to see the world through your child's eyes.

Materials

1. Piece of wire screen
2. Toothbrushes
3. Paints
4. Plain white paper
5. Tape
6. Assorted leaves

Speckled Leaf Art

20

Directions

Tape the plain paper to a flat surface. Arrange the leaves on the paper. Cover the leaves with the piece of wire screen (or mesh) and tape down securely. Mix the paints and put separate colors in paper cups. Dip a toothbrush in the paint and dab on the screen. Use a separate brush for each color or rinse brush before trying a new color. When done, let the paint dry and remove the screen. Lift off the leaves gently and hang the picture on a wall.

Change a
Song

21

Directions

Children like to sing about the familiar things in their lives—family, school, toys, going to bed, mealtimes, siblings, and feelings. Take a well-known melody such as *Twinkle, Twinkle, Little Star* and have your child make up new words to the song. Create many variations. Nonsense words and lots of repetition are fine. Rhyming doesn't matter. Take turns so that everyone has an opportunity to make up a new song.

22 Sunflower Surprises

Materials
1. Packet of raw sunflower seeds
2. Watering can or container
3. Several 3' stakes

Directions
Prepare the soil in a small section of the garden or ground. Put the stakes into the ground about 12 inches apart. At the base of each stake, poke a 1/2 inch deep hole. Plant 2 or 3 seeds in each hole and cover with soil. Water each day. When the plants are 3 feet tall, tie them to the stakes with twine or narrow strips of fabric. When the backs of the flowers turn yellow they are ready to harvest. Cut off the flowers and let them dry out for a few days. Remove the seeds and soak them in salt water for 10 hours. Drain and then spread them on a cookie sheet. Bake at 200 degrees F for an hour. Cool before eating.

Materials

1. Piece of fabric
2. Cord or colored yarn
3. Sewing machine or needle and thread
4. Felt scraps

Mail Delivery

23

Directions

Cut the fabric into a 2' by 1' length. On one half, stitch the letters of your child's name cut from the felt scraps. Fold and sew into a bag. Fold down an inch at the top and hem. Thread the cord through the casing and you now have a bag for your child to carry. With this bag, your child can pretend to be the mailperson. Provide old letters and mailers—use the backsides to indicate where the mail should be sent or delivered.

Clockwork Marching

Directions

In this activity, your child will march to a steady beat—a metronome is ideal or you can clap your hands. Ask your child to march to the beat, swinging arms and lifting the feet. Try slowing down the beat and also making it faster. See how your child adjusts his or her marching to the tempo changes. Halt when the beat finishes.

24

Handprint Plaque

Materials

1. Plaster of paris
2. Aluminum pie dish
3. Water
4. Nails
5. Food color (optional)

Directions

Prepare plaster of paris according to directions. When ready, pour a small amount into the greased pie dish. Lightly grease your child's hand and then press it gently into the center of the dish. Hold it there until the plaster sets—just a couple of minutes. Remove hand and let plaster set completely. A nail can be inserted while the plaster is still moist so the handprint can be hung on a wall. Also try adding food color to the plaster mix at the start. Similar plaques can be made from footprints, elbows, and knees.

26

Earth's Small Treasures

Materials
1. Egg carton
2. Glue
3. Photo of child

Directions

Go on a hike or stroll with your child. As you walk, explain the wonders and miracles of nature...How big trees start from tiny seeds, how rocks are formed, how flowers produce colored petals, etc. Collect some of these "treasures" and when you get home glue them into the recesses of an egg carton. Glue a photo of your child in one also in order to show that he or she is one of nature's treasures too.

Dried Apple Snacks

Materials
1. Small apples
2. String cut into lengths
3. Apple corer

27

Directions
Wash the apples, then remove the core from three or four of them using the apple corer. Thread the strings through the holes in the apples and tie in knots. With the other end of each string, hang the apples outside in the sun to dry (Or apples can be hung from an oven rack. Set the oven very low—150°F). When they are dried, remove the strings, slice, and eat.

Stone Reflections

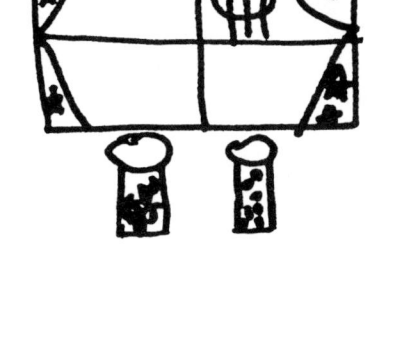

Materials
1. Assorted stones and pebbles
2. Glass jar
3. Bleach

Directions
Gather different colored stones and pebbles with your child. When you get home, wash them and then carefully put them in the jar. Fill the jar with water and add a teaspoon of bleach to keep the water clear. Place the jar where the light catches it and look at the colors that are reflected.

28

Picture Punch

Materials
1. White paper
2. Colored paper
3. Paper hole punch
4. Glue
5. Crayons

Directions

Cut a white sheet of paper in half. Have your child punch holes in it at random or attempt to make a particular pattern using the hole punch. Glue the back of the sheet and place it on top of a sheet of colored paper. Use crayons to enhance the effect of the design.

30

Foam Fun

Materials

1. Can of shaving cream
2. Inflated balloons
3. Paper plates

Directions

This activity is best done outside or in the bathroom. Give your child an aerosol can of shaving cream and some objects to decorate. Look for foam cans with safe, ozone-friendly propellants. Balloons are good to make foamy faces on and paper plates can be used as a base for castles and towers of foam. An outside wall can be used to display foam art or foam can be applied to grass and pavement. Hose areas down when the activity is over.

Farm Visit

31

Directions

Depending on the time of the year, you and your child can make plans to visit a farm. For example, around Halloween and Thanksgiving there are pumpkin farms to visit. Before Christmas there are Christmas tree farms. At other times of the year there are vegetable farms, orchards, dairy farms, flower farms, and sheep or goat farms. Use the telephone to make arrangements and don't forget to dress appropriately.

Materials

1. Fresh flowers
2. Heavy book
3. Cardboard
4. Glue stick
5. Self-adhesive plastic
6. Scissors
7. Newspaper

Pressed Flower Collage

Directions

Open the book and lay the flowers between some newspaper on one of the pages. Repeat on other pages until there are no more flowers to press. Close the book and leave for a few days. When the flowers are dry, remove carefully. Cut the plastic an inch larger than the cardboard. Arrange the flowers on the cardboard keeping them in place with the glue stick. Carefully cover with the plastic. Smooth out the wrinkles and finally trim the edges or fold under.

32

Maraca March

Materials
1. Plastic bottles with long necks, e.g., ketchup and sauce bottles
2. Rice, beans, birdseed
3. Macaroni
4. Masking tape

Directions

Partly fill the bottles with rice, beans, birdseed or macaroni. Seal the bottles with masking tape. Wrap additional tape around necks to make a comfortable handle. Make a pair for each child. Now encourage the child to move and shake the "maracas" either to music or clapping or no sounds at all. Marching is a good activity which can be developed into other locomotions as the child becomes more creative and comfortable with the handheld rhythmic instruments.

Edible Forest

34

Materials
1. Packet of cress seeds
2. Packet of mustard seeds
3. Dinner plates
4. Absorbent paper, such as coffee filter or paper towel

Directions

Place the absorbent paper on the dinner plate. Moisten it completely with water. Sprinkle some cress seeds in a single layer on one half of the plate. Cover with another dinner plate or a saucepan lid to keep the seeds in the dark and leave for three days or until the shoots and roots appear. Keep moist. Sprinkle the mustard seeds on the other half of the plate (they germinate more quickly) and replace cover. When the seedlings are about 1/2" high uncover them and place the plate near a sunny window. Keep moist. When the plants are green, cut with scissors and eat on sandwiches or in salads.

Peek-a-Boo Box

Materials

1. Shoe box with lid
2. Scissors
3. Glue
4. Tape
5. Colored paper, clay, shells, feathers, and odd miniature toys and objects

35

Directions

Cut out a window in one end of the box. Cut out another window in the lid. Inside the box create a scene or a collection of bric-a-brac. Glue or tape objects and pictures to the bottom and sides. Use modeling clay to affix things so that they stand up, such as the feathers. Place the other small objects so that they can be seen through the windows. Replace the lid and look through either window to see the diorama that your child has created.

Action Words

Directions
Introduce these words to your child and both of you do the actions together—STRETCH, LEAP, SLIDE, RUN, CRAWL, FALL, SPIN, and TURN. Now make dances using 2 or 3 of the words, e.g., run, turn, slide. Vary the directions and levels—do the action word backwards or sideways or on the floor.

36

Cylinder Sculpture

Materials
1. Construction paper
2. Fabric
3. Crayons
4. Buttons and beads
5. Yarn
6. Glue

Directions
Lay some paper flat on the table. Cover it with decorative ideas using fabric scraps, buttons, and beads. Attach firmly with glue. Fill in spaces with crayons. When paper is dry, roll it up into a cylinder shape. Glue or staple the ends together. Now stand it on one end and your child has made a cylindrical sculpture.

38 Recycled Mail

Materials
1. Used envelopes—any shape
2. Glue stick

Directions
Collect used envelopes. Ask parents to carefully open their mail so as not to tear envelopes. Glue down the flaps and wait until dry. Now use the backs of the envelopes for scratch paper, lists, painting, drawing, and construction projects. Stamps can be soaked off before gluing and saved for sticker projects or for a stamp collection. Think of other ways to use the recycled envelopes, especially ones with windows in them.

Yum Yum Art

Materials
1. Vanilla instant pudding
2. Shelf paper
3. Food coloring
4. Small bowls
5. Mixing spoons

39

Directions
Mix the instant pudding according to directions. Divide up into 2 or 3 small bowls. Add a different food color to each bowl and stir until blended. Spread out some shelf paper and proceed to use the pudding mix as your child would use finger paints. Create patterns and pictures with the different colors. When your child's hands get messy, she or he can lick them clean.

Mud Play

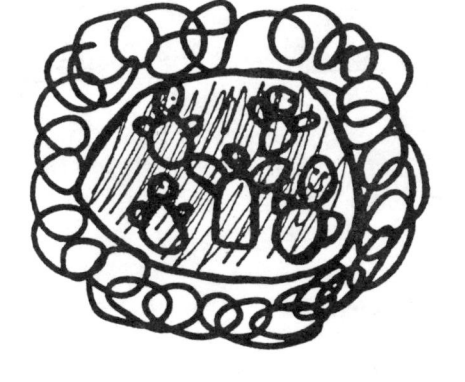

Materials
1. Garden soil
2. Piece of plastic

Directions

All children like the feel of mud. Make a hole in the ground and save the dirt. Put the plastic flat into the hole and fill the hole with dirt and water. Your child can make whatever he or she wants. The objects or sculptures your child creates can be placed on the plastic to dry in the sun. After the activity is over, hose the area down (and your child too!).

40

Paper Chain People

Materials
1. Pencil
2. Paper
3. Scissors
4. Crayons

Directions
Fold paper accordion-fashion so that all sections
are equal. On the top section, draw a person whose hands extend the folds of
the paper. Carefully cut around your person. Open out the paper and your child
will have a chain of several people holding hands. Color them in with crayons
and tape them to the refrigerator.

42

Watery Slide

Materials

1. Large sheet of plastic, e.g., tablecloth or drop cloth
2. Stones or weights
3. Garden hose
4. Lawn sprinkler

Directions

Spread plastic sheet onto the lawn. Weight the edges down with stones or other weights. Plastic sheet may also be stabilized by using tent pins. Place the water sprinkler on one edge of the plastic and attach to hose. Turn water on and when the sheet is completely wet, your child can start sliding and slipping. Keep the plastic wet. Every now and then, move the plastic to another part of the lawn so as not to damage the grass underneath.

Flotation Experiment

Materials

1. Bathtub or sink
2. Lightweight objects — corks, feathers, plastic lids or caps, sponges
3. Heavier objects — paper clips, pencils, buttons

43

Directions

Fill the bathtub or sink with water. Set all the objects nearby within your child's reach. The object of this activity is to see which objects float and which ones don't. Some may float for a while and then sink. Some small objects sink immediately, while some large objects stay floating. Use this experiment to explain to your child the notions of weight and displacement.

Painted Soap

Materials
1. Bar of soap
2. Water-based paints
3. Small paint brushes

Directions

Place soap on a sheet of newspaper. Mix paints and put colors in separate containers (paper cups). Let your child paint directly onto the soap with brushes or her or his fingers. Let the paint dry. The design can be readily washed off and your child can begin another one.

44

Paper Tambourine

Materials

1. Soda bottle caps
2. A nail
3. Strong paper plate
4. String

Directions

Punch a hole in each soda bottle cap with the nail. Take the string and thread two caps together, then tie a knot leaving 6 inches of string. Make slits along the edge of the paper plate. Slide the loose string into the slit and tie another knot so that the string doesn't slip out. Repeat until the plate has about 8 bottle cap units hanging from it. Now it is ready for playing as a musical instrument.

46

Veggie Jungle

Materials
1. Fresh carrots, beets, and parsnips
2. Shallow plastic plate
3. Small plastic animals
4. Small stones or pebbles

Directions
Select 4 or 5 vegetables with little or no foliage. Carefully cut them 1" - 2" from the top. Discard or cook the lower portions. Place the tops in the plate and pour in a little water. Place the plate on a sunny window ledge. In a few days green shoots will appear. Keep water in the plate. Arrange pebbles and toy animals among the sprouting vegetables to make a jungle-like environment.

Dressing Up

Materials

1. Large cardboard carton or wooden crate
2. Old adult clothes
3. Bags, purses, wallets
4. Hats, ties, shoes, belts
5. Scarves, shawls, and other used accessories

Directions

Today is a good day to start a dress up bin for your child. Go through your closet and instead of discarding your old clothes, put some of them in a box or crate for your child to play with. Keep adding to the box as your wardrobe changes. When your child wants to dress up, make available a full-length mirror and have your camera or video ready. Dress up bins provide hours of fun.

Rubber Neck Dance

Directions

While facing your child, identify all the parts of the face and neck that can dance. Try moving the eyes, nose, chin, back of the neck, tongue, and forehead. Now sit in front of a mirror with some rhythmical music on. Dance with the face, head, and neck and see how many dance movements you and your child can make. Experiment with facial expressions too.

48

Fluffy Head

Materials

1. Large paper bag
2. White glue
3. Cotton balls
4. White tissue paper
5. Felt pen

Directions

Place bag over child's head and mark eyes and armholes with felt pen. Remove bag and use scissors to cut out the holes for eyes and arms. Place bag over the back of a chair so that it can be walked around while doing activity. Dip cotton balls into saucer of diluted white glue and then stick each one onto the bag. Scrunch pieces of tissue paper into balls or wads and glue them on top for ears or elsewhere to cover gaps among cotton balls. When the entire bag is covered and the glue has dried, the child can wear it to play in.

50 Natty Napkin Rings

Materials
1. Heavy cardboard tube
2. Water-based paints
3. Crayons
4. Felt pen

Directions

Encourage your family to use cloth napkins at mealtimes. If everyone in the family has his or her own napkin ring, napkins can be used over again and families will save on water and laundry soap. To make individual napkin rings, decorate the outside of the cardboard tube with paints, crayons, or a colorful collage. When completely dry, an adult can slice the tube into 1 inch sections with a sharp knife. Smooth the edges with an emory board. Name each ring with a felt pen, one ring for each person. When ready to use, pull a napkin through the ring starting with a corner and then use at mealtimes.

Cereal Balls

Materials

1. 1/2 cup peanut butter
2. 1/3 cup honey
3. 1/2 cup flaked coconut
4. 2 cups favorite cereal
5. Extras—raisins, dates, banana chips
6. Large bowls

51

Directions

Put the peanut butter, honey, coconut, and extras in a large bowl and mix well. Stir in 1/2 cup of the cereal and put the rest of the cereal in another bowl. Scoop out spoonfuls of the mixture and shape into balls. Roll the balls in the extra cereal. Chill in the refrigerator before eating.

Pet Worm

Materials
1. Glass jar
2. Garden soil
3. Sand
4. Peat (optional)
5. Leaves
6. Live worm

Directions

To make the wormery, put a layer of soil at the bottom of the jar. Add a layer of sand, a layer of peat and finally, a layer of leaves. Place the worm on top of the leaves and then wrap paper around the jar to keep it dark. After a few days, remove the paper and show your child how the layers have begun to get mixed up due to the worm's movements and eating habits.

52

Stringy Gift Wrap

Materials

1. White newsprint paper
2. Water-based paints (tempera)
3. Toilet paper cardboard tubes
4. String
5. Muffin pan
6. Paint brushes

Directions

Mix paints and place several colors in muffin pan with a separate paint brush for each color. Wind string around paper tubes, tying or tucking away the loose ends. Spread the paper on a flat surface and stabilize with thumb tacks or tape. Paint the string on the tubes and while still wet, roll tube over paper until paint is used up. Repaint string with another color and roll again. When finished rolling, wait until the paint is completely dry before removing paper and using as a gift wrap.

54 Flying Saucers

Materials

1. Small Frisbees or plastic plates
2. Popsicle sticks
3. Felt pen

Directions

This game is best played outside with plenty of space. It can be played on the snow, grass, or cement. Throw the Frisbee or plate from a base line and see how far it will fly before touching the ground. Mark the place where it lands with a popsicle stick. Throw again and try to beat the previous record. If more than one child is playing, name or decorate the popsicle sticks, one for each child.

Muddied Waters

Materials

1. 3 clean jars
2. Garden soil
3. Sand
4. Dirt
5. Stick

Directions

The object of this activity is to observe how water gets muddy and clears again. Fill the jars 2/3 full of water. Drop a handful of garden soil in one, a handful of sand in another, and a handful of dirt in the third jar. Watch how the soil, sand, and dirt settle. Stir each jar with a stick. Notice how the water changes color and that each jar is a slightly different color. Now wait and let the jars settle again. Discuss what you and your child observed.

Crinkle Crayon Print

Materials
1. Crayons
2. Paper
3. Newspaper
4. Cold water
5. Paint—black or brown

Directions
Have your child draw a picture or design with the crayons on a sheet of paper. Crumple the paper and dip it in water. Squeeze out the water and spread the drawing to dry on the newspaper. Paint over the drawing. Place another sheet of paper over the top immediately to soak up the excess paint. Separate the sheets of paper and your child will have a lithograph of the original drawing.

56

Wrist Jingles

Materials
1. ¹/₂ yd. of narrow ribbon
2. 6 or more small bells

Directions

Cut ribbon into 6" to 8" lengths. String bells onto ribbon—about 3 bells to each length. Tie knots between bells and at each end of the ribbon. Tie ribbons loosely around child's wrists, but the ribbon should not be able to slip off. Try walking, running, hopping, and jumping and listen to the different jingling sounds that are produced. Also try creating different arm and hand movements for more sounds and rhythms.

58 Grow Your Own Popcorn

Materials
1. 20 popcorn kernels or seeds
2. Liquid natural fertilizer

Directions

Prepare the soil in a 6' by 3' garden spot and make 2 rows about 18 inches apart. Plant 10 seeds in each row 6 inches apart and 1/2 inch deep. Water daily and fertilize once a month. After 3 months, ears of corn will appear on the plants. At 4 months, the tassels will be brown and the ears ready to pick. Have an adult remove the ears of corn with a knife. Pull back the husks to expose the corn. Dry in a warm place for 3 weeks. When bone dry, remove the kernels from the cob by scraping. Store in an airtight jar and enjoy popping your own home grown popcorn.

A Day at the Lake

Materials
1. Sack lunch
2. Long stick
3. String
4. Magnet
5. Small metal objects—
   bottle caps, keys, etc.
6. Blanket

59

Directions
Regardless of the weather, make-believe that you and your child are going on a fishing trip. Prepare sack lunches and gather the other materials. Find a spot inside or outside the house and spread the blanket. Imagine you are by a lake in the woods. To make a fishing pole, tie the string to one end of the stick and tie the magnet to the other. Spread the small metal objects around you. Relax as you fish with your child and eat lunch together.

Fireworks Dance

Directions

Have a discussion with your child about the shapes and sounds of fireworks and about his or her reactions to fireworks displays. Move with your child and shoot into the air with a loud sound then drift down to the ground with a soft sound. Alternate jumping, leaping, and exploding with quiet landings. Encourage the use of arms, legs, and sounds. As a finale, do a dance showing many fireworks going off one after the other.

60

Boxes and Building

Materials

1. Cardboard boxes
2. Masking tape
3. Paste
4. Paint

Directions

With the materials listed and some imagination, your child can build all kinds of objects and buildings. Here are some ideas – trains, boats, cars, spaceships, villages, doll houses, stages, skyscrapers, and space stations. Try creating a scene from a favorite story and then act it out.

62   Bottle Bins

Materials

1. 2 sturdy boxes
2. Colored paper and magazine pages
3. White paper (recycled) or paint
4. Water-based felt pens
5. Paste or glue

Directions

Sort and store glass containers in your home. Decorate the outside of one box with colored paper and pens and the other with white paper or paint. Find a place to keep the boxes, such as in the garage. Start collecting empty glass bottles and jars. Remove the caps and lids and rinse the dirty ones. Place the clear glass bottles in the white box and the colored glass bottles in the colored box. When the boxes are full, an adult can take all the glass to the nearest recycling center. Find more bottles and keep your recycling project going strong.

Bottled Bonanza

Materials
1. Tall glass jar
2. Dry foodstuffs—cereal, beans, lentils, crumbs, seeds, peppercorns, rice, etc.

63

Directions

Layer the foodstuffs one at a time until the jar is filled. The effect should be many colored straight and wavy lines. This activity can be done over a longer period of time by keeping the jar in the kitchen and when there is extra rice or beans, etc., just add them to the layers that are already there. Your child will see the contours grow.

Fall Fun

Materials
1. Leaf rake
2. Child's wagon

Directions
When there is a layer of leaves on the ground, take your child outside for some fall fun. Rake the leaves into small piles and play, chasing around and in between the piles. Or try leaping over them. Using the wagon, cart the leaves to make one big pile. Try to run through it or sit your child in the wagon and pull him or her through the leaves. Try burying each other in leaves, catching the leaves as they fall, and sorting them into colors and shapes.

64

Yarn Holder

Materials

1. Wide cylindrical container with a plastic lid
2. Colored yarn
3. Double-sided cellophane tape

Directions

Wrap tape around the outside of the can starting at the top—but only do a couple of rows at a time. Take pieces of yarn and wind them around the container pressing it into the sticky tape. Repeat until the container is completely covered with rows of yarn. Punch one or more holes in the lid depending on the size of the can. Place a ball or hunk of yarn inside the container and draw the end(s) through the hole(s) in the lid. Replace the lid. If the yarn is to be used for knitting, additional holes can be made for knitting needles.

 # Frogs and Tadpoles

Directions

This is a friendly chasing game played in the swimming pool. The adult is the frog and the child is the tadpole. The frog must keep his or her eyes closed and try to find the tadpole by listening to the splashing and squealing sounds. Once caught, the tadpole can become the frog and the game starts over again. This game can be played in a paddling pool or children can hold onto the edge of the pool while trying to escape the pursuing frog.

Bear Hospital

Materials

1. Old sheeting
2. Masking tape
3. Band-aids
4. Scissors

67

Directions

Tear narrow strips of old sheeting to make bandages. Cut out triangular shapes too. Show your child how to make an arm sling and how to tape down bandages. Using his or her bears, dolls, and stuffed toys as patients, have your child pretend that he or she is in a hospital or clinic where the toys must be treated and repaired. Be careful to handle the toys gently.

Roller Printing

Materials

1. Rolling pin
2. Water-soluble glue
3. Cardboard
4. Cookie tray
5. Paint
6. Paper

Directions

Draw some small shapes on the cardboard. Cut out the shapes and glue onto the rolling pin. Press down the edges until they stick. Mix paint and pour into cookie tray. Tape a sheet of paper onto a flat surface. Roll the rolling pin in the paint and then roll it over the sheet of paper. Let paint dry before removing paper prints.

68

Accompanying the Dance

Materials

1. Toy musical instruments
2. Homemade musical instruments

Directions

Begin this activity by having the child improvise on each and all the musical instruments. The adult can listen attentively or, better still, can dance to the sounds the child is making. Then change roles. The adult plays the instruments and the child dances to them. If there are two children, one can play while the other dances. The sounds of each instrument should suggest the movements and also as the child moves, appropriate sounds should be produced which accompany the dance.

70

Sprout Harvest

Materials
1. Mung beans or lentils
2. Saucer
3. Coffee filter
4. Water

Directions

Place a moistened coffee filter on the saucer. Spread a layer of lentils or mung beans on the paper and sprinkle on a little more water. Place saucer on window ledge and in 2 or 3 days they will begin to sprout. Harvest them in a week to eat raw or put into salads or stir-frys.

Is It a Bird, or a Bat, or a Butterfly?

Materials

1. An old sheet or table-cloth
2. Felt markers or paints
3. Preferably a windy day

71

Directions

Take the old sheet or tablecloth and make it into a large cape for your child. Do this by cutting it to fit and then spreading it out on a flat surface where your child can proceed to put colored markings on it with the paints or felt markers. Attach wrist loops to the corners if your child would find it easier to hold the cape that way. Go outside on a windy day and let your child run into the wind imagining that he or she is a bird, a bat, a butterfly, or anything else.

Freeze and Melt

Directions

Have your child run freely around the space. When you say "freeze" or clap your hands he or she must stop and remain absolutely still. When you say "melt," your child can relax and start to move around again. Continue freezing and melting and encourage your child to try different frozen shapes and to melt in different directions and ways.

72

Streamer Munchkin

73

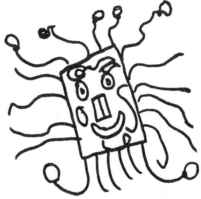

Materials

1. Large paper bag
2. White glue
3. Ribbons, yarn, colored string
4. Bows, rosettes, silk flowers
5. Crayons
6. Colored paper

Directions

Place bag over child's head and mark where eyes and armholes are located with crayons. Remove bag and cut out the holes for eyes and arms. Place bag over the back of a chair so that it is easier to decorate. Cut ribbons, yarn, paper and string into assorted lengths not to exceed the child's height. Now glue the ends of the ribbons, etc. onto the paper bag. Cover front, back, and sides. Attach the bows, flowers, and rosettes last. When glue is dry, place bag over child's head and find a mirror so that child can see the results.

 # Popcorn Packaging

Materials
Popcorn—unsalted and unbuttered

Directions
Popcorn is a safe, inexpensive, and lightweight material to use in packaging. The next time you or your child have to send a precious parcel somewhere, pack it in popcorn instead of paper or styrofoam. Popcorn can also be used when storing or moving glassware, plates, and other breakables. Prepare as much popcorn as you think you will need, allow it to cool and store in an airtight container until ready for use.

Vegetable Dip

Materials

1. Cottage cheese
2. Grated cheddar cheese
3. Dill weed or parsley
4. Worcestershire sauce
5. Salt
6. Assorted vegetables
7. Bowl

75

Directions

In the bowl, put 1/4 cup of cottage cheese, 2 tablespoons of grated cheese, 1 teaspoon of dill or parsley, 1/2 teaspoon of sauce, and a pinch of salt. Mix them all together until blended. Cut or break the raw vegetables into small pieces. Dip the vegetables into the dip and eat.

Rock Crystals

Materials
1. Porous stones or charcoal briquettes
2. Vinegar
3. Salt
4. Warm water
5. Small enamel or glass bowl

Directions

Add 3 tablespoons of salt to a half a bowl of warm water and stir until it dissolves. Keep adding salt until no more will dissolve. Add a tablespoon of vinegar. Fill up the bowl with porous stones or charcoal. Leave on top of refrigerator for a couple of days. Take it down and notice that crystals have begun to form. As the water continues to evaporate, the bowl will be filled with rock crystals.

76

Newspaper Collage

Materials

1. Newspaper
2. Cardboard
3. Colored construction paper
4. Lightweight objects, e.g., buttons,
   corks, matches, etc.
5. White glue

Directions

Attach newspaper to cardboard to make it firmer. Cut out or tear a variety of shapes from the construction paper. Glue these onto the newspaper. Dip the other objects into the glue and attach them onto the newspaper too. Aim at creating a 3-dimensional effect. Colored comic pages can be used instead of construction paper.

78 Wesley Says

Directions

This game is an adaption of "Simon Says" for younger children. It can be played with one child or several. Start by saying, "Wesley says touch your toes," and demonstrate touching your toes. Your child then copies you. After you have done this a few times with simple actions and gestures, let your child be the leader and use his or her own name instead of Wesley. Add a second action, e.g., "Wesley says touch your head and turn around."

Materials

1. Pictures of animals and favorite things
2. Cardboard
3. Glue and scissors
4. Felt markers

Who's Hiding?

Directions

Cut out the pictures of animals and the child's favorite things. Paste them onto squares or shapes of cardboard. On separate cards write the names of each picture, e.g., dog, apple, house, duck, etc. The object of the activity is to teach your child to match the word cards with the picture cards. While your child is watching, turn the picture cards face down and ask "Who's hiding under here?" Your child then tries to guess by placing the matching word card where they think it belongs.

79

Art Exploration

Materials

1. 1" or larger paint brush
2. Large sheets of paper
3. Wooden spoons
4. Dish mop or brush
5. Jar of water-based paint
6. Tape or thumbtacks

Directions

Lay the paper on a flat surface and secure with tape or thumbtacks. Show your child ways to apply paint to paper — brushing, dabbing, flicking, scraping, etc. Encourage your child to experiment with a variety of applicators—brushes, dish mop, spoons, and other kitchen utensils. Your child will explore not only the medium of art (paint) but also the tools of painting.

80

Sounds Alive

Materials

1. Soft objects (e.g., stuffed toys, pillows, slippers)
2. Hollow objects (e.g., pots, cans, egg cartons, plastic bottles)
3. Solid objects (e.g., books, stones, bricks, blocks)

Directions

Different shapes and densities produce different sounds. Make sounds on and with the objects using hands and fingers. Listen to the sounds. Explain to your child that soft sounds and slow sounds are as interesting as loud and fast sounds and that quiet times are as nice as noisy times. Try a quiet time. Close your eyes and listen to the sounds in your thoughts and imagination. Talk about what these sounds are like—soft, loud, slow, or fast?

82 Shoots to Roots

Materials
1. Dried mung beans
2. Cotton balls
3. Small bowl
4. Glass jar

Directions

Soak 5 mung beans (which can be bought at health food stores) in a bowl of water overnight. The next morning, drain the beans and place them on the bottom of the glass jar. Moisten several cotton balls with water and drop them over the beans. Put the jar on a window ledge. After a few days roots will appear and then the shoots. They will push up through the cotton balls and shape themselves in and around the cotton balls accordingly.

Pantomime Play

Materials
1. Old sheeting
2. Masking tape
3. Band-Aids®

83

Directions
Discuss some of the everyday actions your child does, such as drinking milk, brushing teeth, putting on socks and shoes, climbing stairs, etc. Reenact these activities silently and with exaggeration. Make up some other activities to act out. They can be real or imaginary.

Mirror Dancing

Directions

Depending on the size of the mirror, stand or sit in front of one with your child beside you. You can pretend you are on TV. First start dancing with the face and head, moving eyes, noses, eyelashes, etc. Then add the shoulders and neck. Continue to dance with other body parts watching how you both look in the mirror. You may like to try a duet.

84

Toothpick Roadmap

Materials

1. Toothpicks
2. Colored construction paper
3. White glue

Directions

Lay the construction paper on a flat surface and arrange the toothpicks and glue for easy access. The child selects toothpicks and arranges them at will to cover the paper, gluing them down as he or she goes. The toothpicks can form any design, although the 'roadmap' concept may provide a good beginning idea.

Cardboard Stack'ems

Materials
1. Grocery boxes
2. Wooden popsicle sticks

Directions

See how high you and your child can build stacks of cardboard from empty grocery boxes. Save all kinds of boxes, such as those from cereal, crackers, margarine, cookies, and macaroni and cheese. Carefully pry the empty boxes open with a popsicle stick and press them flat. Start a stack on the ground. Place the flattened cardboard boxes on top of each other until the stack is 12 to 18 inches high (or higher!). An adult can tie the stacks up and then take them to the nearest recycling center.

Egg Boats

Materials
1. Hard-boiled eggs
2. Mayonnaise
3. Salt and pepper
4. Toothpicks
5. Paper
6. Tape

87

Directions
Remove the shells from hard-boiled eggs. Cut egg in half lengthwise. Remove the yolk and mix with mayonnaise, salt, and pepper. Cut out two paper triangles for sails and tape them to a toothpick. Put yolk mixture back into egg half and insert toothpick. Arrange several boats on a plate. When hungry, sail one right into your mouth.

Find This Stone

Directions

While at the beach or walking somewhere with your child, play this game. Ask your child to bring you the smallest stone they can find. Next ask them to find the smoothest stone. Continue to send them off to locate stones that are round, speckled, wet, colored, white, too big to carry, etc. Save some of the interesting ones for a rock collection.

88

Smoothy Gift Wrap

89

Materials

1. White newsprint paper
2. Water-based paints (tempera)
3. Spoons
4. Cling wrap
5. Muffin pan or paper cups

Directions

Mix and pour paints into muffin pan or paper cups. Spread paper onto a flat surface and tape it down to keep it stable. Using spoons, dribble and drip paint onto paper, experimenting with different colors. While still wet, place a layer of cling wrap over the paint covering the whole surface. Use hands to smooth cling wrap and create "smoothy" designs underneath. Carefully peel off the cling wrap and allow paper to dry completely before using.

90

Shadow Tag

Materials
1. Playground, park driveway, or lawn
2. Bright, sunny day

Directions
The idea of this game is to try to tag someone by stepping on their shadow. First, have your child find his or her shadow. By changing directions and moving around, see what happens to the shadow. Try to chase the shadow—and lose the shadow. To play tag, whoever is "it" must try to step on another's shadow. When this happens, that child or person becomes "it."

Fire Station Visit

Materials

1. Books and pictures of firefighting and fires

91

Directions

Show your child the books and pictures of firefighting and fires. Explain the responsibilities of the local firefighters and how to call them in an emergency. Call the fire station first to make arrangements and then take your child to visit one. A firefighter will show your child around and answer any questions.

Shadowy Shapes

Materials
1. Large sheets of butcher paper
2. Crayons or felt markers
3. Finger paints

Directions
Go outside on a sunny day and have your child stand on the sidewalk or driveway while you quickly draw the outline of his or her shadow onto the butcher paper. Have your child put his or her body into interesting shapes and trace the outline again. When the outlines are complete, have your child paint them any way he or she wishes.

92

Sanded Blocks

93

Materials

1. Sandpaper
2. 2 wooden blocks or pieces of wood the size of a blackboard eraser
3. Masking tape and ribbon

Directions

Cut the sandpaper so that it fits over the wooden block and overlaps slightly. Tape or tie it securely to the block. Use tacks or thumbtacks if preferred. Make loops out of the ribbon and attach them to the blocks so that your child can hang them from his or her wrists. To make sounds, rub the blocks together. They can be clapped together and tapped too. Play radio or other music and accompany it with the sanded blocks. Remember to keep all your handmade instruments so that when friends are over, you can form a band.

94 Seedy Bird's Head

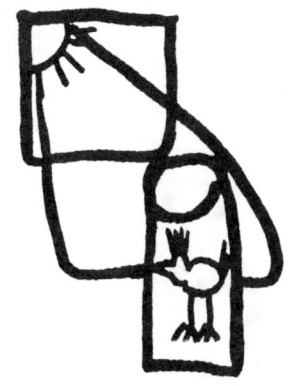

Materials
1. Bird seed—about 3 tablespoons
2. Strong paper towels
3. Rubber band
4. Narrow glass jar
5. Water

Directions
Place the birdseed in the middle of the paper towel. Bring corners of the towel together and tie with the rubber band so that the birdseed is enclosed. Fill the glass jar with water. Place the ball of birdseed on top of the jar with the loose ends of paper towel pushed inside the jar and in the water. After a few days, the seeds will begin to sprout and the ball will look like a bird with a feathered head.

Tiny Yarn Doll Story

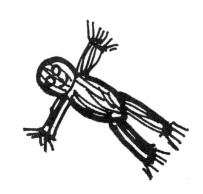

Materials
1. Ball of yarn
2. Heavy cardboard—6" tall
3. Scissors

Directions
Take the cardboard frame and wind the yarn around it 31 times. Slip a piece of string under one end of the frame and tie. Cut the yarn at the other end and remove the frame. Tie a little off at the top to form a head. Remove the original string and detach 2 small clusters to form the arms and tie at the wrists. Tie string around waist. Separate the remaining yarn into two legs. Tie at ankles. Invent a story about the adventures of your tiny yarn doll.

95

Walk Like the Animals

Directions

In this dance activity, your child will try to simulate the ways animals move. Start with familiar animals—cat, dog, duck, and lizard, for example. Say, "If you were a cat, how would you come towards me?" or, "If you were a lizard, how would you move away from me?" Avoid telling your child to move like a certain animal. Instead, allow him or her to sense and create the movements from within. Finally, let your child decide the animal.

96

Clay Sculptures

Materials

1. Clay
2. Paint brushes
3. Molding tools
4. Paints

Directions

Making things out of clay is a challenging and gratifying experience for children. Give the child a lump of ready-mixed and softened clay and let him or her create any kind of object or shape. When it is completely dry (this could take a couple of days) the child can paint it.

98 Family Ties

Materials

1. Pictures from magazines depicting families
2. Family photos
3. Pictures of grandparents and babies

Directions

The object of this activity is to spend time with your child talking about what families are. It is to explain why families love and support each other and how important children are to every family. Show the pictures and photos to your child and encourage questions and comments. Discuss new babies, brothers and sisters, grandparents, single parents, and other relevant topics. Accept your child's opinions and ideas and reinforce his or her feelings of belonging to your family.

Homemade Child's Cheese

Materials

1. 1 quart of milk
2. Saucepan
3. 1 lemon
4. Strainer or sieve
5. Cheesecloth

Directions

Pour milk into pan and cook over medium heat until it just boils. Be careful not to let it boil over. Have your child watch this part. Next add the juice of the lemon and let the milk separate into curds and whey (You might mention the Little Miss Muffet nursery rhyme). Pour through a strainer so that the curds are left behind. Squeeze all the moisture out of the curds by emptying into a piece of cheesecloth, forming a ball and twisting. Chill. Spread on crackers.

Water Races

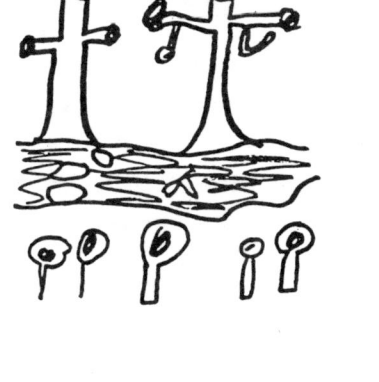

Materials
Sticks, leaves, twigs

Directions
Find a running stream or watercourse. Decide on a starting line upstream and a finishing line downstream. Put floatable objects (stick, twig, leaf, etc.) in the water at the starting line and see which ones reach the finishing line first. If the water flows under a bridge or through a tunnel, drop the objects in where the water enters, then run to the other side or end and wait to see which ones arrive first. Your child will soon be able to tell which objects move faster in the water.

100

Bottle to Vase

101

Materials
1. Soda bottle
2. Colored tissue paper
3. Scissors
4. Newspaper
5. Brush
6. Glue

Directions
Cut or tear the tissue paper into pieces. Mix glue with water (2 parts glue to 1 part water) and brush a thin layer of the mixture onto the bottle. Carefully attach the pieces of tissue paper to the bottle. Brush over with the glue mixture if they will not stick. Continue until the whole bottle is covered. Let it dry completely before using it as a vase. Other objects such as small boxes can be decorated the same way and used to store small toys or trinkets.

102 Balancing Seal

Directions

This activity will show many ways your child can balance on one or more different body parts. Start standing and have your child standing on one foot. Then try one foot and two hands, one foot and one hand. Try balancing on the floor or carpet (e.g., sitting with legs off the floor, kneeling on one knee, on one knee and one hand). Finally, support your child as he or she balances on the top of the head or forehead.

A Morning at Work

Directions

Most mornings children are made aware that one or more adults in the family are going off to work. Make the necessary arrangements to have your child accompany or visit the adult one morning. Show your child around the workplace and explain what goes on. As a result, your child will understand better where the adults go and what they do while they are away from home.

103

Candle Wax Painting

Materials

1. Wax candle
2. Paper
3. Watercolors
4. Paint brush

Directions

Have your child draw a pattern or scene with the wax candle onto a sheet of white paper. The drawing will be almost invisible. When finished, have your child paint the entire sheet with a water color. When the paint dries, the original invisible drawing will show through.

104

Wind Chimes

Materials
1. Medium-size clay flower pot
2. Adhesive tape
3. Colored cord or yarn
4. Nails of varied sizes
5. Scissors
6. Aluminum pie tins

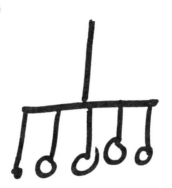

Directions
Cut shapes out of the aluminum—hearts, diamonds, circles—and punch a hole at the top of each shape. String 1 or 2 shapes along 15 inches of cord by knotting. Do the same with the nails. Tape the ends of the cords to the edge of the flower pot and test for sounds and security by holding the pot upside down. Take several lengths of cord and tie a large knot at one end. Pull the free ends through the hole in the pot to make it hang. Tie a strong knot with the ends and place wind chimes in a tree or under an overhang where the wind blows.

106 Pineapple Plantation

Materials
1. Leafy top of a fresh pineapple—1" of flesh
2. Pie dish
3. Sand
4. Perlite from a plant nursery

Directions
Remove the bottom row of leaves from the top of the pineapple. Let plant top dry for two days. Put an inch of sand in the pie dish and sprinkle with water until it is damp to the touch. Press the flat base of the pineapple into the sand. Place the dish in a warm place and water often. When the new leaves sprout, plant can be transplanted to a larger pot. Use one cup of topsoil and two cups of perlite for the potting mixture. Mark a calendar with the date the plantation was started.

Cloud Associations

107

Directions

This activity is to be done on a day when there are clouds in the sky, otherwise find a photography book with photos of the sky in it. Start by explaining how clouds get up in the sky, then take turns pointing out different cloud shapes and patterns. Ask your child what the cloud makes her or him think about and why. Or start putting together an imaginary story about the clouds and the sky. This activity is best when lying on your backs and looking upwards.

Wiggle Waggle Dance

Directions

Play some rhythmic music. Ask your child to warm up her or his body and then start wiggling every part. This can be done standing, sitting or on the floor. After wiggling for a minute, ask your child to NOT wiggle a certain body part, such as the head. Continue to eliminate body parts until only the toes are wiggling. Repeat activity but this time start with one body part wiggling and gradually add all the other parts. Cool down.

108

Wiggle Worm

Materials

1. String or twine
2. Foam plastic egg carton
3. Aluminum foil
4. Toilet paper cardboard tubes
5. Scotch tape
6. Paints and paint brushes

Directions

Paint the cardboard tubes with different colors and let them dry. Cut out two sections from the egg carton. Cut a length of string 2 1/2 ft. long. Link the tubes by threading string through them and tying knots at both ends, then secure it to the tubes. Leave one end of the string long for pulling with. Tape egg carton sections to each end to represent a head and a tail. Scrunch small pieces of foil to make eyes and glue these onto the head section. Pull the worm along and watch it wiggle and roll.

110

Kid's Kompost

Materials
1. Wooden box
2. Used plastic bags
3. Lawn clippings and leaves
4. Vegetable peelings

Directions

Gardens, whether they are in pots or in the open ground, need soil conditioners and extra nutrients. Here is how to make your own compost. Line the wooden box with used plastic bags and place outside in a corner in the shade. Whenever the lawn is mowed save some of the grass clippings and spread them in the box. Alternate the clippings with layers of leaves, vegetable peelings, and other clean organic garbage. Turn over the compost occasionally and soon you will have a rich soil supplement to use in the garden or in the horticulture projects in this book.

Color My Food

Materials

1. Food coloring - vegetable base colors are safest

111

Directions

Most children love to experiment with food coloring. Today let your child color his or her food, the only rule being that he or she must eat what gets colored. Here are some ideas — color the scrambled eggs (blue?), color a glass of milk, paint a slice of bread before toasting it, add a drop of color to a piece of apple, and color the mashed potatoes. Your child will think of others.

Nature's Shadows

Materials
1. White butcher paper
2. Crayons or felt pens

Directions
Go outside with your child on a sunny day. Point out the shadows that trees, leaves, flowers, branches, and shrubs make. These will be on the ground or on a wall. When you find one where the shadow falls on a flat surface, draw its outline onto the butcher paper. Move the paper slightly and draw an overlapping image. When you get home, color in the outlines or leave them be and hang on a wall for viewing.

112

Object Outline

113

Materials
1. Household items with flat bases
2. Large sheet of paper
3. Crayons of felt pens

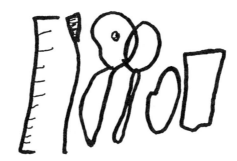

Directions

Spread the sheet of paper on the floor and tape it down. Send your child to search the house for objects to trace around. Place the object on the paper and have your child trace around its base with a crayon or felt pen. Repeat with more objects (return the old ones to their proper places first) until the paper has an interesting design of overlapping outlines.

114

What's Missing?

Materials
1. 6 unlike objects
2. Table
3. 6 similar objects

Directions

Place the 6 unlike objects (such as a toy, a book, fork, article of clothing, slice of bread, and a coin) on the table. While the child's back is turned, remove one of the items. Ask him or her which one is missing. Take away another item and ask which one is missing. Continue until all objects have been taken away. Try repeating the game with similar objects, such as 6 pieces of cutlery or 6 different toys. Work up to 6 different books or 6 dominoes.

Anatomy for Kids

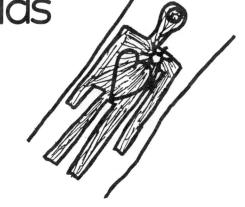

Materials

1. Butcher paper or plain newsprint paper
2. Paints, felt pens, or crayons.

115

Directions

Trace your child's body as they lie face-down or face-up on the paper. Tape the paper in place on the floor. Have your child proceed to draw their body parts on their own outline where they belong, such as nose, ears, fingernails, teeth, hair, and belly button. More difficult parts would include elbows, kneecaps, chin, and heels. For older children, you could label the parts also.

Creative Crayoning

Materials
1. Crayons
2. Paper
3. Paints
4. Paint brushes

Directions

Instead of using crayons for coloring in someone else's pictures, have your child draw whatever she or he wants on sheets of paper. Mix the paints and have your child color in her or his own pictures with the paints. Use brushes or fingers to apply paints. Do not insist on keeping inside the lines!

116

Exploring Sound

117

Directions

Set aside a quiet time when you and your child can sit and listen to the sounds around you. Begin by simply trying to identify what you hear. Distinguish between the sounds inside the house and the sounds coming from outside the house. Or the sounds that are close and the ones that are far away. Also pick out the loudest sounds and the softest sounds. Listen to the sounds of your breathing and of your eyelashes blinking. Share what you hear.

118

Leaf Magic

Materials
1. Healthy begonia leaf
2. 9" square box, 5" deep
3. Peat moss
4. Sand
5. Plastic bag

Directions

Punch holes in base of box for drainage. Fill box to 3" with a mixture of sand and peat moss. Sprinkle with water until damp, but not soggy. Turn the leaf face down and cut through each main vein below where it starts to branch. Make a hole in the soil for the stem. Place the leaf, face-up, flat on the surface of the soil and insert the stem into the hole. Place a clear plastic bag around the box and leave somewhere cool and dry until roots start to grow. Remove plastic bag and transplant begonia in a clay or plastic pot.

Magic Wand

Materials

1. Long stick or dowel
2. Fabric scraps or crepe paper
3. Sequins
4. Gift bow
5. Glue

Directions

Help your child make a magic wand which he or she can use to make spells, make people disappear, and make wishes come true. Wrap the stick in strips of colorful fabric or crepe paper. Glue on some sequins. Attach a gift bow or streamers to the top. Glue more sequins on the top piece. Let it dry. Now the wand is ready for its magical use.

119

Balloon Dance

Directions
Attach air-inflated balloons to short lengths of string. Have your child hold the balloon away from the body and move around it, trying not to get close. Still holding the string, toss the balloon into the air and let it float down. Follow it and copy it. Repeat and have the body go upwards as the balloon is tossed and downwards as the balloon floats down. Holding the string, do turning and wave-like movements with the balloon. Create a dance with the balloon, holding it with both hands.

120

Paper Jewels

Materials

1. Colored construction paper
2. Fine sandpaper
3. Scissors
4. Glue
5. Clear nail varnish
6. Yarn

Directions

Draw a simple shape that your child would like for a jewel. Cut the shape out plus 5 copies of it from the colored paper. Glue the shapes one on top of each other. Wait a day until the glue dries. Using the sandpaper, sand the edges until smooth. Also, sand the top and bottom until the colors show through. The more your child sands, the brighter the jewel will become. Brush the clear nail varnish over it and when the jewel is dry, you can punch a hole through it so that it can be worn as a necklace or ring using the yarn.

122

Sense of Touch

Materials

1. A collection of objects with different textures
2. Photos or pictures of children and people close to each other and nature

Directions

Talk to your child about the sense of touch — how it feels, soft touching, hugging, having hair brushed, etc. Handle the objects you have collected and say how they feel. Look at the pictures of people touching and encourage your child to relate to the closeness illustrated in the pictures and photos. Explain that our sense of touch helps us learn about our surroundings and that being touched and touching gives feelings of love and security.

Crunchy Marshmallow Balls

Materials

1. 5 cups of marshmallows
2. 1/2 stick of butter
3. Breakfast cereal
4. Deep saucepan
5. Waxed paper

Directions

Melt marshmallows and butter over low heat, stirring until blended. Let the mixture cool and then add 3 or more cups of cereal. Stir until cereal is evenly distributed. Have your child wet his or her hands and shape handfuls of the mixture into balls. When molded, place balls on waxed paper to cool and get crispier.

Materials

1. Sand
2. Large, strong paper cup, e.g., one used for shakes
3. String
4. Large sheet of brown or colored paper

Swinging Sand Art

Directions

This activity is best done outside. Make a hole in the bottom of the paper cup. Make another 3 holes around the rim. Suspend the cup by the string by threading the string through the holes and tying it to an overhang or branch. Spread the brown paper below. Now fill the cup with sand and gently push it so that it swings in small circles and arcs. The sand will pour out and make patterns on the paper below. Reuse the sand to repeat the activity.

124

Texture Casts

Materials

1. Modeling clay or playdough

Directions

Work the clay or playdough into a smooth flat shape—like a small pancake. Use the shape to make imprints of different surface textures. Your child presses the shape into the surface and then sees the imprint. A game can be invented to try and identify the surfaces, e.g., sole of tennis shoe, floor mat, outside wall, or tennis racquet.

126

Treasure Hunt

Materials

1. Blank notepaper
2. Felt pens
3. Homemade "treasure," e.g.,
   favorite fruits, small bag of
   old jewelry, matchbox toy

Directions

This activity has to be planned well ahead of time. All clues for finding the "treasure" are to be in picture form. Make drawings of all the places you want your child to search. For example, the TV set, the outside swing, the mailbox, etc. Each clue directs your child to the next clue and so on until he or she finds the "treasure." Creating clues is a lot of fun. Be sure to make the drawings simple and clear. Be prepared for requests to repeat the hunt over and over again.

Taste and Tell

Materials

1. Foods with a variety of tastes—sweet, salty, sour, bland, syrupy, sharp, bitter, rich, and tasteless

127

Directions

The purpose of this activity is to make your child more aware of the sense of taste. Have ready a variety of foods in small amounts. If you like, your child can close her or his eyes while tasting each one. After each food, discuss the taste and whether it is nice or not. Ask your child what are his or her favorite foods and why. Try combining foods of different tastes. What was the taste like then?

Stone Painting

Materials
1. Smooth, flat stones
2. Paints
3. Felt markers
4. Paint brushes
5. Jar of water

Directions
Clean and dry off the stones. Mix the paints and pour into paper cups or muffin pans. Have your child paint the rocks in sequence—while the paint on one stone is drying, apply paint to the next stone. Continue until all stones are colored and dry. Add lines and other designs with the pens. Use the water in the jar to wipe off mistakes and to clean brushes. Painted stones can be used as paper weights or ornaments.

128

Jingle Bell Drum

Materials

1. Oatmeal carton (cylinder)
2. Sturdy string
3. Glue
4. 2 packages of small sleigh bells
5. Colored paper, e.g., wallpaper
6. Tape

Directions

Stiffen one end of the string with glue and let dry. This will make threading the bells easier. String the bells along the string and make large knots between them to keep them apart. Cover the oatmeal carton with colorful paper and glue it on securely. Attach the strung bells to the carton with tape. Wind string in a spiral fashion leaving one or two loops. Now the drum is ready for shaking or tapping and is portable.

130

Pretty Petunia

Materials
1. Petunia seeds
2. Potting mix or garden soil
3. Plastic or clay pot

Directions

Fill pot with soil to 1" from the top. Sprinkle with water until damp, but not soggy. Pick up the petunia seeds with the child's fingers—the seeds are very small—and tap onto the top of the soil. Press down into the soil. Place pot on window ledge and keep moist (with a plastic cover if you like). If there are too many seedlings, thin to about 3 or 4 in the pot. Keep watered and turn pot occasionally so they do not all grow towards the sun. The pretty petunias should bloom in just over 2 months.

Stick Puppets

Materials
1. Old magazines
2. Extra family photos
3. Lengths of thin dowel, popsicle sticks, bamboo, or garden stakes
4. Wood glue

Directions
Find pictures of people who are important to your child— family members, babysitter, teacher, etc. Cut out the person and paste each one onto the sticks near the top. Tell stories with the puppets pretending they are real people. The interactions can be realistic or imaginary, but encourage your child to have and present his or her own ideas.

Yoga Toad

Directions

Practice this activity with your child until you both perfect it. Squat on your heels and balance. Put the palms of your hands on the floor, arms between the knees. Gently rock forward onto the hands lifting the feet off the floor. How long can you balance there? Help by holding your child's hips up. Take small hops forward keeping the arms touching the inner knees or thighs. Avoid putting stress on the knees.

132

Create a Crown

Materials
1. Paper
2. Scissors
3. Glue
4. Crayons
5. Sparkles and glitter

Directions

Cut the paper to look like an open crown shape. Let your child decorate it with crayons, glue, sparkles and glitter. When the decoration is dry, fit it to your child's head and staple or glue the ends together. Play "king" or "queen" for a day and have your child wear the crown. You and your child could make more crowns for the next family birthday party.

134

My Friends and I

Materials
1. Strong cardboard
2. Popsicle sticks
3. Crayons
4. Photos of friends and family
5. Pictures of favorite animals

Directions

Paste popsicle sticks on their edges to form windows on the cardboard. Let dry. Use crayons to color the backgrounds of the windows. Cut around the faces of your child's friends and family and glue them inside the windows onto the backgrounds. Do likewise with the pictures and photos of favorite animals. When your child goes to bed, bring the cardboard display and look at each picture together. Talk about friendship and then close your eyes and send that person love.

Popsicle Parade

Materials

1. Popsicle or icecream sticks (new)
2. Muffin pan or paper cups
3. Popsicle mixture

135

Directions

Prepare a container of popsicle mixture. This could consist of any fruit juice, flavored yogurt, chocolate milk, soda, or Koolaid. Pour the mixture into a muffin pan or paper cups. Put into the freezing compartment of your refrigerator. When mixture starts to freeze, remove from freezer and insert popsicle sticks in each cup. Return to freezer and eat when completely frozen.

Bug Safari

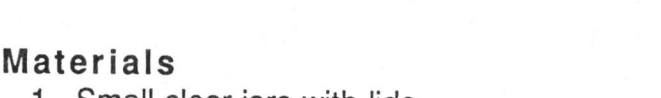

Materials
1. Small clear jars with lids
2. Tweezers or tongs
3. Garden gloves
4. Old spoon

Directions
Plan a walk with your child to the park or woods. Take a backpack with a snack and the small jars and other materials. As you walk, look for insects (under rocks especially) such as ants, spiders, worms, and snails. Use tweezers, tongs, fingers, or gloves to gently pick them up and place into the jars. Be on the lookout for insects which might bite or sting and help your child identify the harmless bugs.

136

Toy Puppet Head

137

Materials

1. Newspaper
2. Paste or glue
3. Paper towel cardboard tube
4. Paints and paint brushes
5. Yarn or cotton balls

Directions

Tightly scrunch a large piece of newspaper into a ball about the size of a baseball. Tear strips of newspaper and dip them into the paste. Cover newspaper ball with wet strips and leave to dry completely. Stuff half a page of newspaper down into the cardboard tube leaving some paper hanging out. Put ball of newspaper inside the excess paper and pull paper up over the ball. Paste paper onto ball and let dry. On the ball, paint facial features. Add yarn or cotton balls for hair. Reinforce cardboard tube with more pasted strips of newspaper to make a handle. Now the puppet is ready for action.

138

Copy Cats

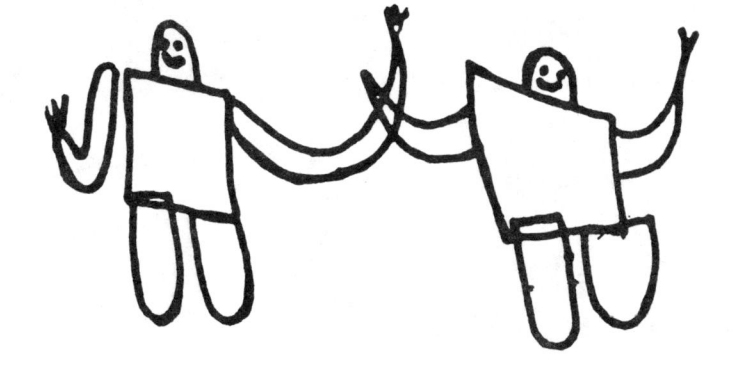

Directions

Stand or sit facing your child and pretend that one of you is a mirror and must do whatever the other one does. Start with slow, simple movements and no surprises. Gradually get more complex and use different body parts. Change roles regularly and encourage creativity and attentiveness.

Mood Swings

Directions

Sit across from your child and explain that you are going to make some faces which tell what mood you are in. Make a variety of faces—happy, sad, worried, surprised, mad, tired, shy, bored, etc. Hold a book or sheet of paper in front of your face between changes. Now take turns with your child to guess what mood the other is in according to the facial expression. This is a good body language activity for both you and your child.

139

Buttermilk
Art

Materials
1. Buttermilk
2. Colored chalk
3. Paint brush
4. White drawing paper

Directions

Paint a thin coat of buttermilk over the drawing paper. While still wet, your child can draw a picture with the colored chalks directly onto the surface. The finished effect is most interesting. Hang somewhere for all to see.

140

Nail Melodies

141

Materials
1. A variety of large and small nails
2. Thread, preferably nylon
3. A tall-backed chair or
   clothes drying rack

Directions

Tie different lengths of thread to the nail heads. Hang the nails from the back of a chair, the rungs of a clothes drying rack, or a stepladder. Nails could also be hung from bathroom towel holders. Use a large nail, fondue fork, or thin dowel to strike nails. Try fast and slow, loud and soft sounds. Other metal objects can be tied and hung for more variety. Use radio music or other music for accompaniment.

142

Hanging Sponge Garden

Materials
1. Birdseed or lawn seed
2. Natural sponge
3. Ribbon or cord
4. Shallow pan of water

Directions

Buy a natural sponge from a drug store or health store. Make a small hole through the center and thread the ribbon or cord through it. Tie a good knot at one end of the cord. Wet the sponge and sprinkle the seed over it and into the air holes. Hang the sponge in a sunny window with the tip of it resting in a shallow pan of water. Seeds will sprout so long as your child keeps water in the pan.

Woman in the Moon

143

Directions
One night when the moon is up, lie with your child on your backs on a blanket or lounge chair in the backyard. Look up at the moon and the night sky. What do you see? Can you connect the stars to make a picture? Can you make out a face on the moon? Imagine what it would be like to be an astronaut flying into space in a rocket. What would you expect to find on the moon? What would you do there? How would you feel about being so far away from earth?

Bridges and Tunnels

Directions

First, discuss with your child the differences between bridges and tunnels—what they typically look like and what they are used for. Make a bridge with your body and have your child go over it. Next make a tunnel and have your child go through it. Take turns creating interesting bridges and tunnels. If there are other children, you can make a series of bridges and tunnels and have the children go over and through them.

144

Pipe Cleaner People

145

Materials
1. Pipe cleaners
2. Twist ties

Directions
Help your child bend pipe cleaners into different shapes. Join some together and make more complex shapes. Use twist ties to assemble several shapes together. This part of the activity is rewarding in itself. Once the child has the skills, then start to make little people with the pipe cleaners. Use the pipe cleaner people to act out a story.

146

Rag Bag

Materials
1. Used clothes
2. Old towels and washcloths
3. Worn-out cloth diapers
4. Old socks

Directions

Growing children are tough on clothes. Instead of throwing clothes away, cut or tear them into good size pieces for use as rags. Hem the ragged edges if desired. Cotton T-shirts and old cloth diapers are best. Old socks are good for dusting and cleaning jobs. Your child can put his or her hand inside and help with the housework. Place the rags and socks in a specially marked bag for use in cleaning jobs and art projects. Make sure the bag is placed or hung low enough for children to reach.

Materials

1. Parfait glass or a tall tumbler
2. Fresh fruit
3. Whipped cream
4. Pudding mix
5. Other edibles, such as chocolate chips, raisins, coconut, nuts, etc.

Yummie Parfaits

147

Directions

Place all ingredients in paper cups or piles ready to go. Have your child layer the ingredients, except the whipped cream, from the bottom of the glass or tumbler to the top. Glass can be tipped to one side for a sloping effect. Add a dollop of whipped cream on the top. Your child could make a few more and provide tonight's dessert for all the family.

Bird Watching

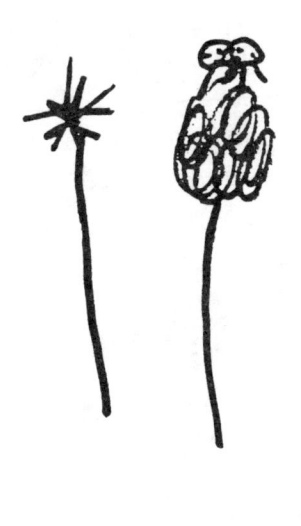

Materials

1. Book about local birds
2. Binoculars

Directions

Check out a library book about the birds of your region.
Spend some time looking through the book together and
identify some of the birds you are likely to see in your area.
Take the book and a pair of binoculars with you when you
go on walks. Watch the birds as they fly or perch. Your child
will enjoy looking at the world through binoculars even
when he or she is unable to find a bird to watch.

148

Leafy Table Mats

Materials

1. Strong colored paper or poster board
2. Self-adhesive plastic or double-sided adhesive tape
3. Leaves and ferns

Directions

After collecting leaves and ferns, press them between newspaper inside a heavy book and leave for a week if possible. Remove the pressed leaves and arrange them on the colored paper which has been cut to table-mat size. Cut the clear adhesive plastic larger than the mats and carefully lay it, sticky side down, over the leaves. Press out all the air bubbles with the hands and smooth the plastic. Finally, trim the edges and the mats are ready to use. Wipe them clean with a damp cloth after meals.

150

Magpie Hunt

Materials
1. Notepaper
2. Felt pens

Directions
Magpies are birds which collect sundry items and hoard them. This game can be played inside or outside. Give your child a list of items which you want found and brought to you. Draw pictures of the items if necessary. Items can range from large ones, such as the Sunday comics to small ones, such as a napkin ring or a soda cracker. Before starting the game, you might like to ask your child to give you ideas for the magpie's list.

Listen to the World

151

Directions

This activity can be done inside or outside. Sit beside your child or back-to-back, and close your eyes. Concentrate on listening to all the sounds around you. Listen to the world. Say what you hear. Can your child identify all the sounds? Are there any soft sounds? High sounds? Take turns saying what sound you can hear.

Squashed Paint Art

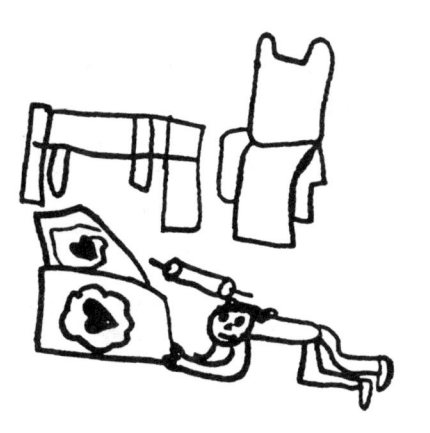

Materials

1. Tempera paints
2. Drawing paper
3. Teaspoon
4. Rolling pin or wine bottle

Directions

Put the paints in a muffin pan or paper cups. Take one sheet of paper and have your child dribble some paint onto it with the teaspoon. Cover this sheet with another sheet of paper. Use the rolling pin or wine bottle to squash the paint. Peel off the top sheet of paper and your child will have a double image of his or her art work. Try this activity with several colors and vary the squashing techniques.

152

Drum Echoes

153

Materials
1. A toy drum or a homemade one
2. Mallet or padded drumstick

Directions

Play a simple rhythm on the drum and have the child listen carefully to it. Start with 3 or fewer beats. Give the mallet or drumstick to the child and have him or her repeat the pattern (or "message"). Continue to listen and repeat the rhythmic phrases. Next, have the child create the original pattern and the adult tries to copy it. Ultimately, each of you have a drum so that the echoing can proceed more spontaneously. This activity can be done without drums by clapping hands.

154 Forever Flowers

Materials
1. Seeds of statice and strawflowers
2. 6 plant containers
3. Potting soil
4. Natural liquid plant fertilizer

Directions
Fill the containers 3/4 full with damp potting soil. Press 4 seeds of each kind of flower in each container and cover with more soil. Label each pot and place on a window ledge. Water daily. After the seedlings are 3 inches tall, thin to one plant per container. Fertilize once a month. Flowers will form and bloom—but not all at the same time. Cut flowers when in full bloom with about 8 inches of stem. Tie the flowers together with string and hang upside down in a dry, dark place. In 3 weeks the flowers will be ready to give to a friend or to place in a vase. These dried flowers do not need water and will last for a long time.

Space Weaving

Materials

1. Yarn
2. String
3. Things to hang

155

Directions

Today you are going to help your child create an imaginary space in his or her bedroom. You could decide on a jungle, a haunted house, a rabbit's burrow, or an inhabitable planet. Start by attaching some yarn or string to the doorknob and then taking it around the room and the furniture. Continue to criss-cross the room until done. Now weave ribbons, scarves, and more yarn in and out of the space. Hang or tie objects which go with the theme.

Elephant Stomp

Directions

Ask your child to describe the characteristics of an elephant—its size, strength, heaviness, and shape. Ask your child to show you how an elephant would move if it was that heavy and big. How would it turn around? How would it get down onto the ground and roll over? How would it move if it was in a hurry? How would it eat apples in a tree? How would it rest if it was tired?

156

A Totem Pole

Materials
1. Egg carton
2. Cardboard
3. Paints or colored markers
4. Glue

Directions
Using the outside of the egg carton, start with the top bumps and paint or color in two eyes. Next cut off a few of the center bumps to allow mouth openings. Leave the other bumps for noses and beaks. Cut a pair of wing shapes from the cardboard and color them too. Glue the wings behind the carton so that they stick out from the sides about halfway down. Cut the bottom straight across so that the totem pole can stand upright.

158

Fingerprinting

Materials
1. Stamp pad
2. White paper
3. Magnifying glass

Directions

Have your child make a set of their own fingerprints on the white paper using the stamp pad. Make a handprint too while their hands are still inked. Wash hands. Make fingerprints of other members of the family. Examine the prints with a magnifying glass and talk about the fact that everyone's are different. Fingerprints are unique to each person. Use this fact to tell your child how special he or she is. Elaborate further to say that everyone is different and therefore they have different talents and traits which we should respect.

Squishy Food Painting

Materials

1. Large zip-lock bags
2. Ketchup
3. Mustard

159

Directions

Put a few tablespoons of ketchup inside a zip-lock bag. Gently squeeze out the air before sealing. Lay the bag flat and smooth the ketchup until it is spread evenly. Have your child draw over the bag with his or her fingers. A drawing will emerge. Erase drawing by smoothing over the bag with palm of hand. Do a mustard bag the same way or mix the ketchup and the mustard together in one bag.

Bark Close-up

Materials
1. Magnifying glass
2. Paper
3. Black or brown crayons

Directions

Explore the trees in your neighborhood. Look closely at the bark with a magnifying glass. Close the eyes and feel the texture of the bark with the hands. Describe it in words. Make a bark rubbing. Take the paper and hold it against the bark. Have your child rub over it with a crayon. Make rubbings of different trees to compare their bark designs. Remember not to peel off the bark of any tree since this will expose the unprotected under layers.

160

Miniature House

161

Materials

1. Small cardboard box
2. Scraps of felt, fabric, and lace
3. Wallpaper remnants
4. Odds and ends from which to make furniture
5. Glue and stapler

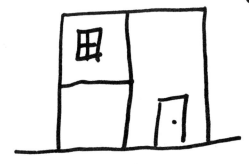

Directions

Divide the box into 2 rooms by using additional cardboard. Line the walls with fabric or wallpaper. Cover the floors with felt or furry fabric. Make small pieces of furniture out of matchboxes, spools, cardboard, etc. Draw windows and doors with felt pens and carefully cut them out. Add lace curtains by gluing or stapling. Continue decorating and furnishing until the miniature house is ready for some inhabitants.

162

Hit or Miss

Materials
1. 3 glass pop bottles
2. Water squirt guns
3. 3 ping pong balls

Directions

Put glass bottles on a box or table. Place a ping pong ball on top of each bottle. Fill the squirt guns with water (it is best to have one squirt gun per child). Have your child stand back a yard or two from the bottles and on a signal from you, he or she tries to knock off a ping pong ball with water from the squirt gun. Modifications can be made with the number of bottles, distance to stand back, number of attempts, etc.

Dad's Turn to Play

163

Directions

This activity involves your child's father or an adult male in the family. Have him invent an adventure story full of excitement and daring. The activity can be played outside or inside and should include climbing, swinging, running, horseplay, and other safe, but physical actions. At first the man should lead the activity, then later when your child gets accustomed to the idea, she or he can lead.

Glue Globs

Materials
1. White glue
2. Waxed paper
3. Colored felt markers

Directions
Spill the glue onto the waxed paper in odd shapes. Let the glue dry until quite hard and clear. Next color the glue globs with the felt markers. Remove the globs from the waxed paper and then hang them in front of a window so the light will shine through them. Glue globs make fine mobiles and make-believe jewelry too.

164

Rubber Band Harps

165

Materials

1. Several rubber bands of many sizes and thicknesses
2. Chair
3. Y-shaped branch or shoe box

Directions

Stretch the rubber bands across the back of the chair or across the branch or around the open shoe box. Now pluck the bands with the fingers and listen to the different sounds. Try holding the rubber band in the middle and plucking. What happens to the sound? Also, try strumming the fingers across all of the bands. The sounds that are produced are typically soft, so make sure the play area is fairly quiet when you do this activity.

166 Avocado Tree

Materials
1. Avocado seed
2. Sharp nail
3. 3 toothpicks
4. Small water tumbler

Directions

Make three holes in the avocado seed with a sharp nail. Insert a toothpick in each hole and make sure they are secure. Fill glass tumbler with water and balance the avocado seed on top using the toothpicks. The tip of the seed should be in the water. Place on a window ledge. Soon a root and a shoot will appear. As soon as the shoot has leaves, snip off the top. This will let the avocado tree branch out. Pot the little tree when roots are thick. Continue to snip off the top growth to make a thicker bush.

Yarn Wigs

Materials

1. Rug yarn—1 skein for a short wig, 2 skeins for a medium wig, 3 skeins for a long wig
2. Scissors
3. Ruler
4. String

167

Directions

Cut the yarn into strands. For the short wig, cut into 2' lengths, medium—3' lengths, and long—4' lengths. Divide the strands into groups of 3. Take a length of string to be the middle part (hair) and tie a large knot at one end. Tie a group of yarn strands around the string and push down to the end knot. Continue until the yarn is gone. Secure the other end of the string. The wig can now be placed on your child's head. It can be braided and clipped to suit.

Touch Twister

Directions

Identify the moving body parts with your child. Choose a part and then try to touch another body part with it, e.g., hand to heel, nose to knee, etc. Do this activity together. Touch a body part of yours with one of your child's, e.g., head to back, elbow to elbow, ear to shoulder. Enjoy the touching, twisting, and learning.

168

Sand Casting

Materials
1. Sand area—preferably outside
2. Stick or piece of dowel
3. Plastic bowl
4. Plaster of paris—about 5 lbs.
5. Large paper clip

Directions
Smooth the wet sand to make a flat surface. Draw your picture or design with the stick making sure the impressions are deep. Toys can be used to make additional impressions. Prepare plaster of paris in the plastic bowl according to directions. Pour quickly onto the sand to fill the impressions and to leave a thickness of 1" to 2" overall. Place a large paper clip into the wet plaster to use as a picture hanger later. Allow plaster to set and then lift the casting out of the sand. Sand casting may now be painted and hung.

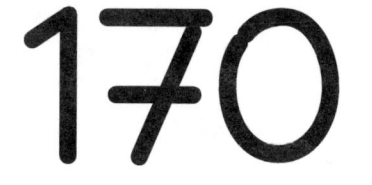

170 Beach Beautification

Materials
Garbage bag

Directions
Beaches can quickly become spoiled by litter. On your next outing to the beach, take along a garbage bag, preferably a burlap sack. Decide on a strip of beach to walk along. As you walk, pick up all the garbage that is lying on the sand and drop it into the sack. At the end of your "beach beautification" walk, empty the sack into a garbage bin. Save the sack for your next visit to the beach.

Grandma's
Granola

Materials

1. 2 1/2 cups oatmeal
2. 1/2 cup coconut
3. 1/2 cup almonds or nuts
4. 1/2 cup grapenuts
5. 1/2 cup margarine
6. 1/2 cup honey or sugar
7. 1/2 cup raisins or dates

171

Directions

In a large bowl mix together (with hands) oatmeal, coconut, almonds, and grapenuts. Melt the honey and margarine and stir into dry ingredients. Spread evenly on a cookie tray and bake at 300 degrees F for 20 minutes, stirring frequently. Remove from oven and fold in the raisins. Cool. Store in an airtight container or eat immediately. Makes 1 pound.

How Many Insects?

Directions

Take your child for a walk in the park, a meadow, or by the sea. See how many insects you can find. Look among the plants, gently lift up rocks, and poke around damp leaves. Tell your child the name of the insects and what they eat. For younger children, the adventure is in the search. It is surprising how many different insects can be spotted during a walk in natural surroundings.

Me in the World

Materials

1. Large piece of paper
2. Glue
3. Scissors
4. Crayons

Directions

Go outside and gather small flowers, leaves, pebbles, twigs, and other small objects and foliage. Clean them off and then glue them onto the paper. When the glue is dry, you and your child can fill in the empty spaces around the objects with drawings of your child's world, that is, his or her house, yard, family members, pets, etc.

174 Fun Obstacle Course

Materials
1. Old tires or hula hoops
2. Jump rope or tow rope
3. Laundry baskets
4. Cardboard cartons
5. Chair or stool

Directions

Outside or in the garage, set up an obstacle course for your child using equipment from the house and yard. Your child should have obstacles to go under, over, through, around, inside, and outside. Colored yarn or chalk can be used for your child to follow. Aside from the materials listed above, you could have your child go under a rug, hop along a ladder on the ground, and swing from a rope. Once the course becomes familiar, your child could try it moving backwards or could be timed.

The Electric Show

Materials

1. Hair comb
2. Small pieces of paper
3. Balloon

175

Directions

To create a static electricity field, have your child run the comb through his or her hair a few times. Then try to pick up the pieces of paper with the comb. Next, blow up the balloon and tie it. Rub the balloon a couple of times against your child's arm or leg. Now put the balloon against a wall and note how it sticks there. Explain to your child the properties of static electricity and give other examples, e.g., lightning.

Newspaper Leaf Prints

Materials

1. Assorted leaves
2. Saucers
3. Paints
4. Newspaper
5. Plastic soda bottle

Directions
Pour small amounts of paint into the saucers. Spread a sheet of newspaper on a flat surface. Dip each leaf in the paint and place it paint-side down on the newspaper. Repeat until several leaves are arranged on the paper. Cover arrangement with another sheet of newspaper. Use the soda bottle to roll over the top. Remove the top layer of newspaper. Carefully remove each leaf and your child will have a set of colorful leaf impressions.

176

177

Bottle Tooting

Materials
1. Empty glass bottles with narrow tops
2. Water

Directions
Pour different amounts of water into each bottle. To make the bottle "toot," blow straight across the open top. Try short breaths and long breaths. Alternate short and long breaths. Hold the bottle against lower lip and see how long your child can "toot." You and your child can make duets, or you can have others participate to form a "tooting" band.

178

Orange Grove

Materials
1. Seeds from an orange or another citrus fruit
2. Plastic or clay pot
3. Potting soil
4. Popsicle sticks

Directions

Remove seeds from an orange or another citrus fruit, such as a lemon, tangerine, or grapefruit. Fill the pot with dampened potting soil. Press 3 or 4 seeds into the soil. Write the name of the fruit on the popsicle stick and the date and then put the pot in a warm, dark place until the seeds germinate. Bring into the light and take care of your orange grove by watering frequently and turning the pot occasionally to encourage the seedlings to grow straight and tall.

I Am A Fish

Materials

1. Blue construction paper
2. Photo of child's face
3. Glue
4. Sand
5. Brushes
6. Tape
7. Crayons or felt pens

179

Directions

Create a story about living and swimming at the bottom of the sea. Prepare the bottom of the sea by brushing glue onto the blue paper. Sprinkle sand on the paper and wait until glue dries. Pour off excess sand. In one of the spaces, glue your child's photo. Using crayons or felt pens, draw a fish's body and tail connected to the photo. Have your child draw other sea creatures and seaweeds. Use more blue paper if necessary. Finally, make up the story and share it.

High Space,
Low Space

Directions
Go outside with your child and talk together about the space around us. Distinguish between "high" space up in the sky, "low" space (down on the ground), and "medium" space (in the middle). What living things move in these spaces? Ask your child how she or he would move in high space, low space and middle space. Experiment with dance movements and have your child explore the space above and below.

180

181

Paper People Cutouts

Materials
1. Cardboard
2. Black felt marker
3. Construction paper
4. Scissors
5. Colored markers or paints

Directions
Using the black marker, draw an outline of your child onto the cardboard and fill in some basic features. Cut it out carefully. Draw different outfits with colored paper or wrapping paper using the cut out person as a guide. Put tabs on the shoulders and waists of the clothes so they can be attached. Cut around the outfits. Add features and accessories with the markers or paints. Use magazine pictures too. Outfits should be easily attached and removed and have variety.

182 Family Time Capsule

Materials
1. Strong, sealable container
2. Family mementos
3. Daily newspaper
4. Photos of the family

Directions
Fill the container with a collection of family items which represent each member of the family. Have your child choose what he or she considers important or valuable. Put everything in the container and add the day's newspaper and photos of everyone. Seal the container and attach a note to the outside saying when the container is to be opened—10, 20, or 30 years away. Finally, put the container in a safe place.

Cheese Balls

Materials
1. 6 tbs. grated cheese
2. 2 tbs. soft butter
3. 10 tsp. flour
4. 10 tsp. Rice Krispies®
5. Bowl
6. Cookie tray

183

Directions

Grate the cheese into the bowl. Add butter, flour, and rice krispies to the grated cheese. Stir until evenly blended. Form into little balls and place on a greased cookie tray. Bake at 375 degrees F for 10 minutes. Cool before eating. These are nice dipped into ketchup.

Bird Feeder

Materials
1. 1/2 gallon milk carton
2. String
3. Crayons or paints
4. Bird food—seeds, nuts, dried bread, dried fruit

Directions
Cut out large windows from all 4 sides of the milk carton, leaving 2 inches, top and bottom. Color with crayons or paints. Poke 2 holes through the top of the carton. Tie the string through each hole. Fill the bottom of the carton with bird food. Finally, take the feeder outside and hang it by the strings from a tree. Remember to frequently replace the bird food with a fresh supply.

184

Colored Crayon Balls

185

Materials
1. Old and broken crayons
2. Used plastic sandwich bags
3. Twist ties
4. Muffin pans

Directions
Peel the paper off the old crayons and break them into small pieces. Select a group of several different colors and place them in the sandwich bag. Seal tightly with a twist tie. Put several bags of crayon pieces in the muffin pan. Place the pan in the sun or in a slightly warm oven for 20 minutes or until the crayon wax is soft. It should never be hot. With the crayons still in the bags, shape into balls. Drop the bags into ice cold water. Remove the firm balls from the bags and use to color with.

186

Materials
1. Treasure items, such as
   fresh fruit, small toy, a book

Directions

Sit on the floor with your back to your child and your eyes closed. Have a small "treasure" or prize hidden behind your back. Your child goes to the back of the room away from you and begins to tiptoe towards you, making no sound. If you hear a sound, turn around quickly and open your eyes. If you see your child move, he or she goes back to the start, otherwise your child must "freeze" until you turn to the front. Continue until your child has sneaked up behind you. When your child reaches you, you can reward him or her with the treasure.

Heads and Faces Collage

Materials

1. Old magazines
2. Plain paper
3. Glue
4. Scissors
5. Crayons or felt pens

187

Directions

Go through the old magazines with your child and find pictures of heads, faces, hair, glasses, earrings, and hair pieces—anything having to do with the head. Cut them out, then glue them onto a sheet of plain paper to form a collage. If parts of the faces or heads are missing, have your child draw the missing parts with crayons or felt pens. As you work, identify and name everything.

Confetti Eggs

Materials

1. Raw eggs
2. Confetti
3. Fingernail scissors
4. Crayons

Directions

Take the scissors and cut a small hole at one end of the egg and a larger hole at the other. Remove the insides of the egg by blowing through the small hole over a bowl (Use for cooking). Decorate the outside of the egg with crayons. Fill the inside with the confetti and tape the holes closed until ready to use. When the moment is right, your child can crack his or her egg over someone's head and watch the reaction!

188

Snare Drum

Materials

1. Empty cookie or cake tin
2. 20 paper clips
3. Cardboard
4. Masking tape

Directions

Remove the lid from the empty tin. Turn the tin upside down and set the paper clips on the recessed bottom. Cut a piece of cardboard the same size as the tin bottom (use the lid to trace around). Place it over paper clips and secure with masking tape. Use chopsticks or pencils to play on the cardboard.

190

Parsley Patch

Materials
1. Packet of parsley seed
2. Cup of water
3. Clay or plastic pot
4. Potting soil

Directions
Soak the parsley seeds in the cup of water overnight. Moisten the potting soil and lightly pack into the pot. Drain the water off the seeds and drop the seeds onto the soil in the pot. Sprinkle some potting soil over the top of the seeds. Place pot in a sunny place. Once the parsley is a couple of inches high, thin to make healthier plants. Use parsley leaves in salads, soups, whipped potatoes, and sauces.

Sidewalk Shadows

191

Directions

Do this activity in the early morning or late afternoon sun. Stand on the sidewalk or on the driveway with your child and together construct shapes that make interesting shadows. Try to make buildings, cars, animals, trees, etc., by collaborating with your child. When you have a shape, try moving it a few steps. Make it larger or smaller. Think of other variations and ideas.

BAND-AID®
Dance

Directions

For this activity, your child takes one body part and attaches it somewhere on his or her body. For example, put the hand on the hip or the elbow on the wrist of the other arm. Let your child experiment with the ways he or she can stick one body part onto another. Try moving with the parts stuck to each other. While your child is dancing you can both sing, "I am stuck on BAND-AID® and BAND-AID® 's stuck on me." Also, try attaching body parts to another person and dancing together.

192

Tub Sponge Sculptures

193

Materials
1. Assorted sponges
2. Scissors
3. Water resistant glue, such as
   Elmer's Stix-All®

Directions

Cut the sponges into geometrical shapes. Involve your child in deciding which pieces to use to build interesting shapes, such as boats, ice cream cones, a house,etc. Glue the pieces together. Let the glue dry completely before playing with the shapes in the bathtub.

194

Military Shower

Materials
1. Soap
2. Washcloth

Directions

Your child can use water sparingly in the shower and still get clean and refreshed. Turn the water on just long enough to wet the whole body and the washcloth. Take the soap and lather the washcloth. Close eyes and wash face first and then the rest of the body. When your child is covered with lather, turn on the shower again and simply rinse off. Hair shampoo can be applied after the body is lathered and then rinsed clean at the same time.

Food Sculpture

Materials

1. Cheese spread—cream cheese, sour cream, onion soup mix
2. Bowl
3. Snack foods—chips, pop, corn, pretzels, crackers

Directions

Prepare the cheese spread by warming 3 oz of the cream cheese until it is soft. Blend in 3 tablespoons of sour cream and mix in 1/2 packet of soup mix. Arrange the snacks in piles and then proceed to build a sculpture, selecting from the assortment of snacks and cementing them together with the cheese spread. The cheese doesn't add a lot of strength so it is best to keep the sculpture low. When finished, your child can have fun eating his or her creation.

195

Nature Walk Collage

Materials
1. Old magazines
2. Poster board
3. Scissors
4. Glue or paste

Directions

Talk with your child about what he or she might see on a nature walk. Go through some old magazines together and find pictures of some of these things—trees, fields, streams, animals, flowers, etc. Cut them out and arrange on the poster board. Glue each picture down. This can be an on going project with the collage growing as your child finds more pictures that fit the theme.

196

Animal Collage

Materials

1. Old magazines (e.g., National Geographic)
2. Poster board
3. Scissors
4. Glue or paste

Directions

Go through the magazines with your child and find pictures of animals. Cut them out and then have your child arrange them any way he or she wants on the poster board. Glue or paste the pictures down. When the glue is dry, hang the collage on the wall at your child's eye level. Help your child learn the names of the animals by frequently identifying them.

198 Animal Travel Game

Directions

Make up a nonsense sentence about animals traveling. For example, "A turtle rode the bus to school today." Your child then responds with a sentence that is just as silly using another animal and a different mode of transport. You reply with another sentence such as, "A cow rode a bicycle to school today," and continue until you both feel like stopping.

Backwards Day

Directions

Today you are going to turn your child's day around! Everything that happens at the start of the day, will take place in the evening, and vice versa. Begin the day with a bedtime story and a bath, take the afternoon nap in the morning and have breakfast at night. Think of other things that you could do in keeping with a "backwards" day. Do not forget to let your child know what's going on and ask him or her for ideas.

199

Mirror Image Painting

Materials

1. Drawing paper
2. Thick tempera paints
3. Paint brush

Directions

Fold the paper in half and then open out flat. Have your child paint on one half of the paper only. When the painting is done, fold the paper along the crease line and press the two sides together. Open the paper to discover mirror images. Repeat on a fresh sheet of paper using more than one color.

200

Sounds Like?

201

The idea of this activity is to imitate with the voice the everyday sounds we hear. It can be done inside or outside the house — just walk around and listen. Try imitating such sounds as a door shutting, the telephone ringing, the washing machine or drier, the teakettle whistling, the fire crackling, and the fridge humming. Repeat outside with sounds such as birds chirping, leaves rustling, sirens, brakes squealing, and planes overhead. Who knows, you might have a sound effects person in the making!

202

Spring is Here

Materials
1. 6 daffodil bulbs or 6 crocus bulbs
2. 5" clay or plastic pot
3. Potting soil

Directions
Moisten the potting soil and half fill the 5" pot with some soil. Place the bulbs on the soil and then add more soil until the tips of the bulbs just peek through. Sprinkle with water and set the pot somewhere cool and dark. Check the bulbs every couple of days and keep moist. After 3 weeks they will have roots and green shoots. Bring them out into the sunlight and continue to keep the soil moist. After a month they will bloom and it will seem as though spring has arrived. Bulbs will grow faster if kept in the fridge for a week or so before planting.

Magic Movies

Materials
1. Adding machine tape—
   use the backside of used tape
2. Matchbox
3. Crayons

203

Directions
Ask your child to draw a story along the tape. It should look somewhat like a comic strip. A series of shapes or pictures would work too. Cut out a square in the side of the matchbox to serve as the viewing area. Thread the tape through the box so that the child's pictures appear in the window. Place the box on a table and wind and unwind the tape through the box.

Rope Shaping

Directions

Find a jump rope or a length of cord. Make a simple shape with it on the floor. Ask your child to put his or her body into the same shape. Repeat with interesting shapes. Now reverse the order of the activity. Have your child make a shape and then try to duplicate it with the rope. This is a good activity for other family members to join in since sometimes it takes 2 people to complete the shape of the rope.

204

Paper Chains

Materials
1. Colored construction paper
2. Scissors
3. Glue, paste, or stapler

Directions
Cut paper into 1" x 4" strips. Glue or staple ends of first strip to make a ring. Thread next strip through this ring and glue ends together. Continue threading the strips through the previous rings until the chain reaches the desired length or you run out of paper. The chain can be hung on the Christmas tree or for birthday parties.

206

Stream Clean-up

Materials
Garbage bag

Directions
Streams and creeks can become spoiled and polluted by garbage. Take the family for a walk or picnic near a creek or stream. Bring along a garbage bag, preferably a burlap sack. Patrol the stream bank and pick up all the garbage that can be found. Take the garbage home in the sack and dispose of it in a trash can. Try to reuse the bag. Remember, if you take your dog along with you, his waste should be picked up too.

A "Cool" Cake

Materials

1. A plain cake
2. Vanilla or white icing
3. Food coloring
4. Corn syrup
5. Chocolate syrup
6. Spatula and spoons
7. 5 paper cups

Directions

Spread the icing over the cake as smoothly as possible. Pour 2 tablespoons of corn syrup into each paper cup. Next, add a different food color to each cup and add chocolate syrup to one. Drip the colors onto the cake using spoons. Let the colors run together or mix them up and experiment with patterning. For an interesting birthday cake, wait until the guests are seated and pass the iced cake around for everyone to help frost.

207

Puddle Walk

Nothing feels better on a warm day than walking through puddles with bare feet. Hold hands for balance and make big splashes and little splashes. Jump from one puddle to the next. Observe how the water ripples and moves. See your reflection in the puddle before walking through it. Return the next day to see if the puddle is still there or if it has grown larger. On colder days wear gumboots or old shoes. Change shoes when you and your child get home.

208

Terrific Foil

Materials
1. Aluminum foil and cardboard
2. Liquid soap
3. Q-tips and paint brushes
4. Paints
5. Soft-tipped nail

Directions

Tape a sheet of foil to the same size piece of cardboard. Mix a few drops of liquid soap with the paint. Brush paint over the foil and then let it dry. Use a nail with a soft point to scratch a design or picture. Be careful not to scratch too hard, or the foil will tear.

210

Rolling Pins

Directions
Find a grassy slope in a park and make
sure there are no tree stumps or sharp
objects in the ground. This could also be
attempted on a snowy slope, provided the child is wrapped warmly and doesn't mind
having a little snow on his or her face. Climb to the top and lie parallel to the slope with
hands and legs stretched out and together. Gently push off and roll down the slope like a
rolling pin. See how far you can go before slowing to a stop.

The Shape of Things to Come

Materials

1. Plain paper
2. Crayons or felt pens

211

Directions

Ask your child to name some things that use circle shapes, such as a ball, a dinner plate, or the wheels of a truck. Then have her or him describe what would happen if a truck wheel was square or if a beach ball was triangular. Finally, have your child draw a picture of one or more things you talked about, such as a bicycle with square wheels.

Chalky Watercolor

Materials
1. Colored chalks
2. Drawing paper
3. Liquid starch
4. Paint brush

Directions
There are two ways your child can make a chalk watercolor. The first way is to draw a picture with the chalks on the drawing paper and then brush liquid starch over it. The second way is to dip the paper in the starch to start with and then draw a picture with the chalks on the wet paper. Either way, when dry, these pictures look beautiful.

212

Bongo Drums

Materials

1. 3 different size cylinders
2. Masking tape
3. String

Ponk
Ponk
Ponk

Directions

Tape and tie the cylinders together to make a set of drums. Set the drums on the child's lap and briefly demonstrate how to beat each drum with the fingers, palms, knuckles, and heels of the hands. Oatmeal cartons of different sizes are perfect for this activity.

214

Outdoor Terrarium

Materials
1. 2 or 3 wide-mouthed jars
2. Vegetable and flower seeds
   —dwarf varieties
3. Fertilizer
4. Garden or planter space

Directions

Wash and dry the jars and remove any labels. Locate a small piece of garden or an empty planter. Remove weeds and stones and dig over the soil. Mix in a little fertilizer. Sow the seeds in an area no larger than the size of the mouth of each jar. Space jars about 12" apart. Cover seeds with soil and sprinkle with water. Place jar over the seeds and watch them germinate inside their terrarium or hothouse. The jars protect the seeds from extremes of temperatures. Remove jars to water the seedlings. When the seedlings are strong and healthy, remove the jar permanently.

Lion Mask

Materials

1. Empty cereal box
2. Egg carton
3. 1 sheet of black paper
4. 1 sheet of white paper
5. 3 broom straws
6. Paints—yellow, black, and orange

215

Directions

Cut away one end and the back of the cereal box. Cut out diamond shapes for eyes. Cut 2 ears out of the white paper and staple onto the top of the box. Paint the box and the ears a yellowy-orange. Remove a pocket from the egg carton and paint it black. Attach it to the middle of the box for the lion's nose. Draw on a lion's mouth and freckles. Staple on the straws for whiskers. Finally, cut the black paper into strips and curl. Attach to top to form lion's mane. Make up a jungle story and play the lion's part.

Leggy Dance

Directions
Play some bright, rhythmical music. Stand facing your child and point out the different parts of the legs and feet. Now discover all the ways each part can move (e.g., bend the knees, wiggle the toes, circle the ankles, arch the foot, kick, and hop). Dance on one leg and dance with both legs. Add other body parts when child is ready—head, arms, shoulders, back, and waist.

216

Bag Building Blocks

Materials
1. Paper grocery bags
2. Newspapers
3. Tape—masking or packing

Directions
Lay the paper bag flat on the floor or a low table. Fold the top over about 6" - 8" and crease the bag on the fold. Open the bag and fill it with scrunched up newspapers, one sheet at a time. Fold the bag on the crease line and securely tape the bag closed. Bags may be painted or decorated before or after filling and sealing. These blocks are great for building forts, castles, tunnels, and towers. Recycle bags and paper when finished.

218 Wild Bird Snacks

Materials
1. Unshelled, unsalted peanuts
2. Apple and orange peels
3. Yarn or string

Directions
Your child can provide wild birds with snacks without having to own or build a bird feeder. Tie lengths of yarn or string around individual unshelled peanuts. Hang them from the branches of a tree. Apple peels and orange peels can be tied with yarn and hung up, too. Try other natural snacks that can be secured with string and hung outdoors.

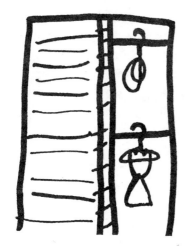

Orange Pomander

Materials

1. 2 or 3 oranges
2. Box of whole cloves
3. Colored string

Directions

Cut oranges in half and remove pulp without disturbing the skin. Fit the halves back together again by placing one inside the other to make ball shapes. Secure the halves by inserting cloves through both layers of skin. Insert more cloves in the orange skins, in patterns if desired. Tie colored string around the balls so that they can be hung from a closet rod. These pomanders will give a delicate scent to your clothes for many months.

219

Ants On Parade

Materials
1. Ants
2. Magnifying glass
3. Crackers

Directions
Have you noticed how children love to watch ants? When you discover a trail, take the magnifying glass and look at the ants close up. Notice that they have 3 separate body parts—head, thorax, and abdomen. Count the legs. Place cracker crumbs in the path of the ants and watch the ants carry them away. Ants are social insects and help each other work together. Notice, too, how they meet and greet each other. Follow them until they go out of sight.

220

Spoon People

221

Materials

1. Plastic spoons
2. Cotton balls
3. A few pipe cleaners
4. Felt pens
5. Construction and tissue paper
6. Scissors and glue

Directions

To make little people or puppets out of the plastic spoons, first glue on the cotton balls for hair and/or a beard. Twist pipe cleaners around "neck" of spoon to form arms. Use felt pens to draw on facial features. Finally, create clothing from the paper, attaching with yarn or string. Collaborate with your child to produce a story or play with the spoon people as characters.

222 Button Pitch

Materials
1. Assorted buttons
2. Masking tape

Directions

Make a line on the floor with the masking tape parallel to and about 3' from a wall. Give your child and any other children 10 buttons each and have them stand behind the tape. Take turns pitching the buttons against the wall so that they fall and bounce on the floor. The goal is to have the buttons land as close to the wall as possible. To compete with another child, after each round of pitching, the child whose button is closest to the wall, picks up both buttons. Keep playing until one child has all the buttons.

Color Grouping

223

Directions
Ask your child to look at the things in his or her room and group the things by the different colors. Which things are red, white, green, etc.? Ask your child what his or her favorite color is. Also ask which colors go together best. Finally, ask which colors are "warm" colors and which colors are cold.

Finger Touch-ups

Materials
1. Drawing paper
2. Colored chalks
3. Liquid starch

Directions
Have your child make some drawings on the paper with colored chalks. Provide her or him with a theme or an artistic problem to solve. When the drawings are finished, ask your child to dip her or his fingers into the liquid starch and go over the chalk marks. There may be some smearing at first, but in the end the touched-up drawings will appear more interesting than the originals.

224

Clapping Rhythms

Directions

Try this rhythmic game with your child. All you need is some space and a low noise level. As your child walks around, clap each time he or she takes a step. Encourage your child to run, hop, jump, gallop, and skip, and continue to clap out the rhythm his or her steps make. For a change of perspective, have your child clap out the stepping rhythms that you make—but be sure to keep them reasonably slow, regular, and simple.

226

Mr. Potato Head

Materials
1. Medium size potato
2. Pipe cleaners
3. Toothpicks
4. Modeling clay

Directions

Scrub and then dry the potato. Break the toothpicks (about 6 of them) in two. Take the modeling clay and shape into noses, ears, mouths, eyebrows, and eyeballs. Use several colors. To create a potato head, push the blunt end of the toothpick into one of the clay shapes. Now insert the sharp end into the potato at the place where your child thinks it should go. Continue attaching the clay facial features until the head is complete. Use the pipe cleaners to make arms and legs. Mr. Potato can have different faces according to your child's imagination.

Stand Up Drawings

Materials

1. Poster board or used cartons or boxes
2. Pencil
3. Crayons
4. Scissors

227

Directions

Have your child draw some simple shapes, such as trees, houses, people, and animals. When you cut them out, leave a space beneath each drawing. Fold the shapes at their bases and stand them up. Have your child arrange the stand-up drawings into a scene for a make-believe story. Participate in the story and be prepared to add more shapes as the story evolves.

Silly Walks

Directions

First of all, ask your child to walk around in his or her normal, everyday walk. Now try walking very high, very low, very wide, very narrow, very fast, and very slowly. Think of other ways people walk and try them out. Now ask your child to create his or her own special walk and make it as silly as possible. Can you do your silly walk backwards? sideways? turning? Finally, slow down your silly walk until it stops in an unusual shape.

228

Tot's Table Arrangement

Materials
1. Paper plate holder
2. Dried gourds, corn cobs, etc.
3. Paper, silk, or plastic flowers
4. Small toys and figures
5. Playdough® or plastic clay

Directions
Explain to your child that together you are going to make a table decoration for the home. You could make a sample one for him or her to follow, or simply set the materials on a sheet of newspaper and let him or her create one. Place dollops and dabs of the Playdough® or clay on the paper plate holder to keep the decorative pieces in place. When it is finished, place the arrangement someplace special so family and visitors can see it.

230

Bug
Treats

Materials
Apple cores

Directions

Bugs are tiny, but they play a very important role in keeping the earth healthy. Protecting them and feeding them is beneficial to everyone. Bugs should be moved to safety if they are on a sidewalk or playing area. Bugs like to eat organic garbage. Save your apple cores and place them in the garden or in corners of the yard. Soon the apple core will disappear. Bugs often feed at night, so have your child check every day to see how much of the apple core is left.

Pancake Art

Materials

1. Pancake batter
2. Frypan
3. Butter
4. Spatula
5. Soup spoon
6. Small bowl or cup

Directions

Mix the pancake batter with milk to make it slightly thin. Pour some into a small deep bowl or a cup. Melt butter in the frypan and when it is evenly spread, remove the frypan to the bench. Have your child take spoonfuls of batter and drip it into the frypan to form a design. Return the frypan to the heat. When the design starts to turn brown, pour more batter over it. Cook until the edges are dry and flip over. The design will be embedded. Finish cooking and serve.

231

Rainbow Color Coding

Materials
Samples of paint colors
found at hardware or
paint stores

Directions
Ask for paint color samples at your local hardware store.
Select mainly primary colors, pastels, and browns and
greens. The idea is to have your child match the color
samples with plants, flowers, and natural things in his or her
environment. Going outside with a handful of color samples
is a good way to teach your child to recognize colors and
associate them with living things.

232

Cork Boats

Materials
1. Assorted corks
2. Straws
3. Toothpicks
4. Playdough®
5. Lightweight paper

Directions

Weight the undersides of the corks with Playdough® Cut sails from the paper and use the toothpicks as masts. Attach the sails by poking the toothpicks through the paper. Set the cork boats in water and adjust the Playdough®so that they sail upright. Propel the boats along by blowing through the straws. If using a large bowl of water, conduct races to see who can blow their boat from one side to the other.

234

Splash Splash

Materials
1. Shallow swimming pool
2. Beach ball

Directions

This activity is good on a hot day. Have the children stand around the pool with the beach ball. They try to make each other wet by throwing the ball hard at the water. Do not throw the ball at each other, just at the water. If there is just one child, he or she can play the game with an adult.

Evaporation Experiment

Materials

1. 2 clear plastic cups
2. Felt marker
3. Clear plastic wrap
4. Water

235

Directions

Part fill the plastic cups with water so that they both have the same level of water. Mark the levels with the marker. Seal one of the cups with plastic wrap. Leave for a day. Look at both cups and mark where the water levels are if they have changed. Do this for a few more days. Your child will notice that the water level goes down in the cup that has no cover. Where does the water go? Talk about the water disappearing and explain what evaporation is.

Transparent Triumph

Materials

1. Newspaper
2. Drawing paper
3. Black felt marker
4. Crayons
5. Oil—baby or cooking
6. Rags

Directions

On the drawing paper, have your child outline a design or picture with the black marker. Color in parts of it with the crayons. Turn the drawing over and lay it face down on the newspaper. With the rag, rub oil on the back of the drawing paper. It will become instantly transparent. Hang the artwork in the window so that the light can shine through.

236

Finger Tapping

Ding dong
dunk donk
dink jonk

237

Materials

1. 10 thimbles or acorn caps
2. Small BAND-AID®s
3. Old pair of children's gloves
4. Buttons

Directions

Place the thimbles or acorn caps on your child's fingers. To make sure they fit snugly, secure with the small BAND-AID®s. Begin tapping with the fingertips on a table or a non-carpeted floor. Now experiment with other surfaces—stone, metal, bone, marble, plastic, formica, ceramic. Listen to the different sounds that each surface produces. If you have an old pair of children's gloves, you can glue larger size thimbles onto the ends of the fingers or simply sew buttons on. Then you will have permanent "finger tapping" gloves for your child.

238 Chives for the Kitchen

Materials
1. Chive bulbs
2. 5" used clay or plastic pot
3. Potting soil

Directions

Moisten the potting soil and fill the pot to 1" from the top. Do not pack down. Press 5 - 10 bulbs into the soil and cover with more potting mix. Pat down. Place pot on window ledge in the sun and watch the shoots appear. Small purple flowers will appear too. Snip off the green leaves to flavor soups, stews, salads, and baked potatoes.

Early Indian Weaving

Materials
1. V-shaped branch
2. Yarn or string
3. Nature walk collected objects—feathers, shells, grasses, flowers, roots, etc.

Directions
Make believe that you and your child are early Indians and go for a nature walk. While you are walking talk about early Indian life and collect objects that the Indians may have found too. Find a fallen V-shaped branch and wrap the string or yarn around the branch to make a loom. Weave, hang, and tie in the objects that you found. Take the branch home with you for family and friends to admire.

239

Amazing Maze

Directions

Use masking tape (if you are inside) or chalk (if you are outside) and trace a maze for your child to follow. Include shapes, such as triangles, squares, circles and ovals. Instruct your child to use different steps while following the maze. These could include running, walking on tiptoe, hopping, and crawling. When your child comes to a shape he or she could perform a solo dance inside before proceeding along the amazing maze trail.

240

Self-portrait Puzzle and Gift

241

Materials

1. Large photo of your child
2. Cardboard
3. Contact cement
4. Scissors

Directions

Cut the cardboard the same size as the photo. Cement the photo to the cardboard. Turn it over and on the cardboard side, draw jigsaw puzzle lines—straight lines are best. Cut along the lines. Let your child reassemble the pieces to form his or her own picture. Put puzzle pieces in a bag and give to another family member to try. Send the puzzle to grandparents as a gift. Write a message on the back of the puzzle if desired.

242

I Believe Wallpaper

Materials

1. Drawing paper
2. Crayons or markers
3. Scissors
4. Tape

Directions

This is an ongoing activity which can be used to decorate your child's bedroom. Start by asking your child to draw pictures of important things in his or her life. Suggestions are:1) loved things, 2) valued things, 3) hopes and dreams, 4) beliefs. Attach the pictures to the bedroom wall where a border would be appropriate, near the ceiling is a possibility. Add to the border as your child completes each drawing.

Apple Plumps

Materials

1. Large apples—one for each member of family
2. Baking tray
3. Apple corer
4. Butter
5. Brown sugar
6. Fillings—raisins, dates coconut, nuts, etc.

243

Directions

Remove the core from each apple with the corer and sprinkle the inside of the apple with some sugar. Set the apples in a greased baking tray. Stuff the centers of the apples with the filling, pushing down firmly. Pour a little warm water into the tray, just enough to cover the bottom. Bake for 30 - 45 minutes at 350 degrees F. Every now and then, baste the apples with the liquid in the tray. Remove apples from oven and eat when cooled.

Caterpillar to Butterfly

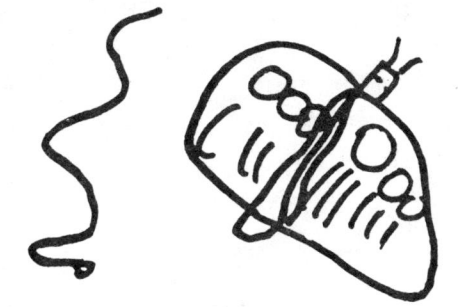

Materials
1. Picture books and magazines
2. Photos of the family
3. A picture book showing growth stages of humans, such as *The Family of Man*
4. A book about butterflies

Directions
Take the books and look at pictures of all the ages and stages of human growth. Explain how all living things grow and change. Compare photos of family members from childhood until adulthood. Explain that, unlike humans, caterpillars grow and change into butterflies. This is called "metamorphosis." Look through the butterfly book and point out the changes from egg to adult. Go outside and see if you can find some caterpillars and butterflies.

244

Bag Lady Doll

245

Materials

1. Paper grocery bags
2. Construction paper
3. Crayons
4. Yarn
5. Pieces of fabric

Directions

Lay one of the bags flat and have your child draw the face of their doll. Glue or staple several lengths of yarn to form hair. Use fabric pieces or colored paper to make a bow or turban for the hair. Cut strips of paper from one of the other bags to make arms and legs and glue these to the "face" bag. More fabric can be used for feet and hands. Attach these with glue or staples. Construct and add other accessories from fabric or construction paper.

246

Turtle Races

Materials
1. Cardboard
2. String
3. Crayons or markers
4. Sturdy glass tumbler

Directions

Trace a circle on the cardboard with the glass tumbler as the outline. Draw a turtle's head and legs. Add a tail. Color in both sides of the cardboard turtle, then cut it out. Make a small hole in the turtle's head and thread 12" of string through it. Tie the other end of the string to a table leg, about 10 inches from the ground. Start with the turtle close to your fingers. Pull the string taut and watch the turtle stand. Release the string and the turtle will flop forward. Keep repeating this action until the turtle reaches the table leg. Make another turtle and have a race.

Steamy Experiment

Materials
1. Teakettle
2. Metal saucepan lid
3. Water

247

Directions
Boil water in the teakettle. Turn heat to low when water boils. As the steam comes out of the spout, hold the saucepan lid in front of it. See that your child notices how the steam turns into water once it touches the lid. Recount how the water in the kettle turns into steam and then turns back into water again. Find other examples of condensation for your child to notice, such as drops of water on the bathroom window, breath on cold glasses, etc.

Blurry Art

Materials
1. Drawing paper (water-color paper is best)
2. Water-based paints
3. Cookie tray
4. Water
5. Paint brushes

Directions
Fill the cookie tray with water. Dip a sheet of drawing paper in the water and hold it up to let the water drain off it. Lay it on some newspaper and while it is still wet, apply the paints with paint brushes. Watch the blurring effect of the wet colors on the wet paper. When the paper is dry, your child can add detail with felt pens or crayons.

248

Musical Jar Xylophone

249

Materials

1. 10-12 empty glass jars or bottles
2. Homemade "drumsticks"
3. Pitcher of water
4. Food colors (optional)

Directions

Arrange the jars or bottles on a flat, low surface (e.g., an ironing board). Pour water into the jars in varying amounts and add drops of food color. Provide the child with a selection of "drumsticks" and encourage him or her to explore the various sounds and rhythms that can be produced by tapping the jars.

250 Crocus Garden

Materials
1. 8 - 10 crocus bulbs
2. Empty ice cream carton
3. Potting soil

Directions

Cut 8 - 10 holes in the sides of an ice cream carton. Poke smaller holes in the base for drainage. They should be about 1" in diameter. Carefully pack the moistened potting soil into the carton and each time you come to a hole in the side, place a crocus bulb near it. Press the soil down firmly to keep it from spilling out of the holes. Leave 1" to spare at the top. Place the carton in a cool dark place for 6 weeks, checking weekly to see that the soil is moist. Bring the carton into the sunlight and allow the green leaves to protrude through the holes. The crocuses will bloom in about a month.

Tent Time

Materials

1. Blankets
2. Furniture

251

Directions

Before you start this activity, remove all precious ornaments and potted plants from the room. Provide your child with 3 or 4 blankets and facilitate the construction of a huge tent. Drape the blankets over the furniture. When the tent is finished, encourage your child to play a make-believe game, such as being in a circus, a haunted house, a fort, or a magic forest.

Circle Dancing

Directions

Identify with your child all the things in and around the house which are circular. These may include wheels, plates, balls, clock faces, coins, cookies, and door knobs. Roll a coin and a ball and watch them travel. Have your child put his or her body into a round or circular shape. Encourage your child to move in circles and explore the ways round objects move in place and from place to place. Try spinning and swirling too.

252

Coat Hanger Mask

253

Materials

1. Wire coat hanger
2. Old nylon stocking
3. Fabric and felt scraps
4. Yarn
5. Glue

Directions

Manipulate the coat hanger until it is in a rounded shape. Cut nylon stocking in half and pull lower (footed) half over the coat hanger. Tie around the neck with the yarn. Cut out eye and mouth shapes from fabric and felt pieces. Glue onto the stocking. When finished, your child can hold the "mask" in front of his or her face and act out another personality.

254

People are Good

Directions

This activity is an opportunity to talk with your child about the goodness all people have inside them. Ask your child to suggest some ways to be kind to others and to respect all people regardless of how they look, talk, and live. It is important to build your child's trust and tolerance. Make a game of imagining what another person's life is like. For example, someone who is handicapped. Talk about the goodness that person has inside, the fun things they might like to do, and how your child should try to see the good in others.

Wagon Train

Materials

1. Celery
2. Carrot
3. Toothpicks
4. Peanut butter

255

Directions

Wash celery and cut into 2 inch lengths. Scrub carrot and cut into slices. Attach 4 round carrot slices to celery with toothpicks to make little wagons. Fill each wagon with peanut butter or a soft cheese. Admire, then eat.

Night Hike

Materials
Flashlights

Directions
Plan a night hike with your child. The child's world looks very different at night. It sounds different too. Let the child carry a flashlight also and hold hands with him or her. While the adult keeps the path well-lit, the child can look around with his or her own light. Every now and then stop, turn off the flashlights, and look up at the moon and stars. Keep a cheerful conversation going and don't go too far from home.

256

Papier-Mâché Balloon

257

Materials

1. Newspaper
2. Balloon
3. Flat dish or pan
4. Paints and paintbrushes
5. Paste—wallpaper or wheat
6. Yarn or rubber band

Directions

Mix the paste until it is thin and creamy, then pour a little into a flat pan. Tear the newspaper into narrow strips 6 - 8 inches long. Have lots and lots of them. Blow up the balloon and tie it tightly with the yarn or a rubber band. Dip the newspaper strips in the paste and apply to the outside of the balloon. Cover balloon entirely and then repeat with 2 or 3 more layers. Smooth surface with hands and wipe off any excess paste. Allow the paper to dry completely before decorating with paint and paint brushes.

258 Who Remembers?

Materials

1. Photos of a family trip, a birthday party or a visit to the zoo.

Directions

In this activity, your child is encouraged to remember as much as possible about an important event in his or her life, preferably in the right sequence. The photos are for jogging the memory. Give plenty of hints to help the story along and paraphrase from time to time to keep the sequence on track.

Energy From the Sun

Materials

1. 3 used cans with the labels removed
2. White water-based paint
3. Black water-based paint
4. Brushes
5. Thermometer

259

Directions

Paint the outside of 2 of the cans—one with white paint, one with black paint. Fill each can with the same amount of water (use a measuring cup) from the faucet. Place the cans on a sunny window ledge or in the sun somewhere. Let them sit for about 3 hours. Now take the temperature of the water in each can. Which can contained the warmest water? Why was this so? Explain to your child the principle of solar energy and its benefits.

Dip and Dabble Art

Materials
1. Paper towels or napkins —coffee filters are OK too
2. Muffin pan
3. Food coloring
4. Water

Directions
Mix the food coloring with some water in the muffin pan so your child has 3 or 4 colors to choose from. Fold the paper any way your child wants, then dip the corners briefly into the colors. Let the paper dry before unfolding, otherwise it might tear. Experiment with different folds or try crumpling the paper before dipping it into the colors. Press the papers flat and mount on cardboard.

260

Copy Cat Music

261

Materials

1. Musical instruments with notes—
   flute, xylophone, harmonica, or
   guitar

Directions

Sit back-to-back with your child. Play a few notes on the instrument. Ask him or her to hum
or sing them back to you. Start with familiar nursery rhymes, Christmas songs, or
well-known jingles if you can play them; otherwise a group of notes is fine. After a while,
give your child the instrument and see if you can copy the notes that he or she produces. If
you do not have access to musical instruments, sing the notes and phrases with your own
voice.

262 Potted Lilies-of-the-Valley

Materials
1. Pips of a Lily-of-the-Valley plant
2. Clay or plastic pot
3. Potting soil

Directions
Obtain the pips from the roots of a Lily-of-the-Valley plant where they grow or from a nursery. They are shaped like small bulbs. Fill the pot with potting soil to about 2" from the top. Plant the pips about 2" apart and cover all but the tips with more potting soil. Set the pot in a well-lit place and keep it cool and moist. In a few weeks the lilies will be about to bloom. The flowers are small, white and very fragrant.

Switching Roles

263

Directions

This activity requires that you and your child switch roles for the day (or part of the day). Explain to the rest of the household what is happening and ask their cooperation. If more convenient, your child could pretend to be another member of the family—a sibling or grandparent. The make-believe could include duties, clothes, behaviors, vocabulary, and other habits. Keep the activity positive and fun.

Inside-Outside Moves

Directions
Illustrate the difference between inside and outside with a real or an imaginary box. Have your child get inside and explore the movements that are possible. Next have your child move outside the box staying close to it. Alternate between inside moves and outside moves. Try moving only the hands inside the box, then only the hands outside the box. Repeat with feet, head, and one leg. Finish with all parts in or all out.

264

Fancy Dress Hat

Materials

1. Old hats—straw, felt, or fabric
2. Artificial flowers
3. Feathers and bows
4. Ribbons and old lace
5. Fabric remnants
6. Glue

Directions

Begin creating an interesting hat by covering the brim with fabric remnants and attaching them with glue. Next attach the flowers, bows, and feathers. Wrap the ribbon and lace around the center and tie a bow in the back. Add more bits and pieces to the hat until the desired effect is achieved. Put on the hat and go find a mirror!

266

Flea Trap

Materials
1. Pan of water
2. Dishwashing soap

Directions

Most fleas live in the rugs and carpets of houses and not on your child's pet dog or cat. Your child can make a flea trap by filling the pan with water and adding a teaspoon of dishwashing soap. Place the pan of water on the floor under a lamp. Fleas are attracted to the light and will jump into the water and drown. Empty the pan regularly and refill with the soapy water.

Ice Bowl

Materials

1. Medium size ball
2. Cooking oil
3. Deep foil pan
4. Pastry brush

Directions

Scrub the ball clean and then paint it with vegetable oil. Place the ball in the foil pan. Fill the pan with water to 1/2 inch from the top. Now place the pan and ball in the freezer compartment overnight. The next day, remove the ball and the foil pan and your child will have an ice bowl in which to put ice cream or a frozen dessert. Bowl can be reused by rinsing and returning to the freezer.

267

Rain Gauge

Materials
1. Clear glass jar
2. Nail varnish (red)
3. Ruler

Directions
On the outside of the jar, have your child mark regular intervals with nail varnish. She or he can use the ruler or some other measure—it doesn't have to be in inches or centimeters. Place the jar outside where it won't be knocked over. After each rain, see how much rain filled the jar. Empty the jar or keep an ongoing record of how much rain has fallen.

268

Career Dolls

Materials

1. Cardboard
2. Construction paper
3. Scissors
4. Glue
5. Crayons

Directions

Adult should first trace or draw some different body shapes onto cardboard—male and female. Add facial features and hair. Discuss with your child the different careers or jobs that people have. Then let him or her decide which ones will apply to the cardboard shapes. Using construction paper, scissors, and glue, outfit the cardboard dolls appropriately. For example, dancer, chef, doctor, builder, farmer, etc.

270

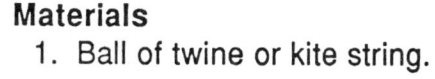

Spider's Web

Materials

1. Ball of twine or kite string.

Directions

Tie one end of the string onto a doorknob or other protrusion. Walk the ball of string anywhere in the room looping it around the furniture and other stable fixtures until the space is criss-crossed with string. A good rule to make is that the string must not be wound around anything that might break or fall over. This activity may also be done in the yard on the playset or among a group of small, sturdy shrubs.

Babies Collage

Materials
1. Old magazines such as *Parenting, Child, Working Mother* or *Parents*
2. Scissors
3. Glue or paste
4. Cardboard

271

Directions
This activity is ideal for children who are expecting a baby sister or brother. Go through some old magazines with your child and find pictures of babies and the things that babies need, such as diapers, bedding, toys, clothes,etc. Cut them out and then you and your child can arrange them on the piece of cardboard like a collage. Glue the pictures onto the cardboard and then hang the collage where your child can see it often and talk about it.

Bubble Paint

Materials
1. 1/2 cup Ivory flakes
2. 1/2 cup water
3. Mixing bowl
4. Food coloring
5. Baby food jars
6. Drawing paper

Directions
Beat the Ivory flakes and water until thick. Pour small amounts into the baby food jars and add a few drops of food coloring to each jar. Have your child use the bubble paint as finger paints on some drawing paper. Let the picture dry overnight.

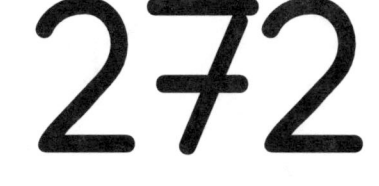

272

Zoo and
Farm Sounds

273

Materials

1. A story about visiting the zoo or a farm from a storybook, or make one up as you go along

Directions

Read the story to your child and explain that each time an animal is mentioned you will stop reading for a moment while he or she makes the sounds of the animal. Read it a second time through and this time have your child sing the animal sounds.

274 Miniature Greenhouse

Materials

1. Large glass jar with wide mouth and screw-on lid
2. Gravel or small pebbles
3. Empty tuna fish can
4. Hammer and nail
5. Plant seedlings

Directions

Using hammer and nail, poke 3 holes in the bottom of the can. Put one layer of gravel or pebbles in can and then fill with garden soil (or potting mix). Moisten the soil. Carefully transplant the seedlings into the soil. Place the taller plants in the middle of the can and the shorter ones around the outside. Now put the tuna can with the plants on top of the jar lid. Invert the glass jar and screw in onto the lid. Place your miniature greenhouse in indirect sunlight and water when the plants start to wilt. Replace seedlings which die or become too tall.

My Own Story

Materials

1. Notebook
2. Pen or pencil
3. Crayons

275

Directions

In this activity, your child will think of a story and while she or he tells it to you, you will record it in a notebook. Leave every alternate page blank for your child's illustrations which she or he can draw after the story is complete. Read the story back to your child and be prepared for additions and elaborations. Save the book of stories for when your child is older.

A B C Shapes

Directions
Review the letters of the alphabet that your child knows and recognizes. Start with the most familiar letter of the alphabet and have your child make the shape of the letter with his or her body. It helps to show your child a picture or example of the letter first. This is a good activity with another child since many letters need two bodies to complete.

276

Paddle Boat Voyage

Materials

1. Scrap block of wood: 4" x 8" x 2"
2. Thin strip of wood: 2" x 3" x 1/4"
3. 2 long nails
4. Rubber band—small and thick
5. Hammer

Directions

Hammer the 2 long nails into one end of the block of wood, just far enough so that they can't be pulled out. Test the rubber band to see that it stretches tightly across the nails. Place the thin strip of wood inside the rubber band and wind it round and round. The piece of wood is the paddle for the boat. Hold the paddle still while the boat is placed in the bathtub or sink. Release the paddle and watch the paddle boat move through the water.

278 Family Calendar

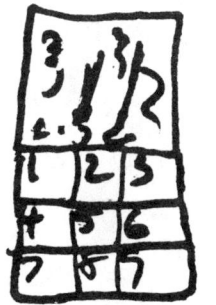

Materials
1. Butcher paper or poster board
2. Markers, crayons, or paint
3. Stickers

Directions

This is a good monthly activity to do as a family. An adult can draw up a large monthly calendar on the paper or poster board. Each family member is represented by a colorful sticker and the family as a whole can be represented by another symbol, a gold star, for example. As the family plans its monthly activities and appointments, the children can apply the stickers accordingly. As new events come up, be sure to add the appropriate stickers. The adults, can of course, write in the details around the stickers.

Surprise Salad

Materials

1. Raw vegetables
2. Slivered almonds
3. Large pkt. lemon gelatin
4. 1 cup cottage cheese
5. 1/2 cup mayonaise
6. Large, deep cake pan

279

Directions

Cut vegetables up into small pieces—strips, cubes, florets, wedges, etc. Arrange them in a pattern on the bottom of the cake pan. In a bowl, dissolve the gelatin in 1-1/2 cups of boiling water and add 1 cup of cold water. Carefully spoon 1/2 cup of the gelatin over the vegetables. Put cake pan in the refrigerator. Meanwhile, beat the cottage cheese and mayonnaise into the remaining gelatin. When the vegetable gelatin is firm, spread the other mixture over the top. Chill.

Weather Diary

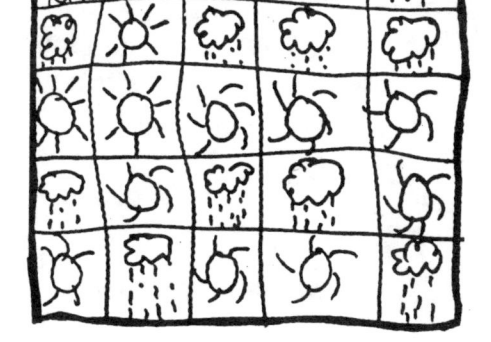

Materials
1. Notebook
2. Pencil
3. Crayons

Directions

In a notebook help your child to keep a visual or graphic record of the weather. Perhaps after breakfast each day you could both draw what the weather looks like outside. Use symbols for sunny, rainy, cloudy, etc., or have your child make a picture each time. Write in the date and whereabouts. When your child is ready, he or she can take over all the entries.

280

3D Picture Frame

281

Materials

1. Paper grocery bag
2. Coat hanger
3. Photo of child or other family member

Directions

Turn paper bag upside down. Cut a square or round opening in the bag about a foot down from the base. Cut another small hole in the center of the base to hang the hanger on. Tape the photo to the inside of the larger opening and check to see that it is visible and lined up. Take the coat hanger and put it inside the bag. Pull the curved handle through the smaller hole and hang the 3 dimensional frame somewhere where it can be seen.

282 Bobby Pin Ball Game

Materials
1. Bobby pins
2. Waxed paper
3. Strong cardboard
4. Small objects to be used as balls—buttons, beans, or marbles

Directions

Find a square of cardboard, such as the back of a writing pad. Cut 3 quarter-size holes in the cardboard. Rub the waxed paper over the surface to make it slippery. Stick the bobby pins around the edges of the holes to form traps. With a felt pen, draw a wide path from the top of the cardboard to the bottom circling the holes. The object of the game is to place a button or bean at the start of the path and, by moving the cardboard, try to guide it to the end of the path without falling into the traps. Hold the cardboard in both hands.

Feely Box

Materials

1. Large cloth bag or pillow-case
2. Assortment of toy animals and familiar objects
3. Rubber band

Directions

Without your child watching, choose 3 or 4 toys and objects that belong to him or her (e.g., hairbrush, teddy bear, shoe, and toy truck). Place the objects in the bag and tie the open end with the rubber band. Ask your child to guess what the objects are by feeling the bag. Remove the object when the guess is successful and continue until there are no objects left. Take turns enclosing objects and guessing what they are.

283

Customized
Light Switch

Materials

1. Light switch plate
2. Acrylic paint
3. Small brushes

Directions

Replace your child's light switch plate with a customised one that your child has created. Get all the materials ready. Using the small brushes, have your child paint on a design or picture and his or her name. Wipe mistakes off with water. Let the plate dry completely before screwing back on the wall.

284

Child's Own Operetta

285

Directions

With your child, make up a make-believe story which involves animals, nature sounds, and favorite storybook characters. As you tell the story together, sing some of the words and have your child make all the sound effects. Include movements which seem appropriate and fun too.

286 Rows of Radishes

Materials

1. Packet of radish seeds
2. Outdoor garden plot
3. Hand shovel and fork
4. Thick stick

Directions

Find a small area of the garden and begin by preparing the soil. Your child first removes stones, weeds, and other debris. Turn the soil over with the shovel and crumble it in the hands so that it is fine. With the stick, your child next draws several straight lines. Sow the radish seeds in the rows (about 1/2" deep) and cover with soil. Sprinkle the rows with water and pat them down firmly. In less than 3 weeks, the radishes will be ready to harvest. Wash thoroughly before eating.

New Endings

Materials
1. Favorite storybooks

Directions
The object of this activity is to read a familiar story to your child and change the ending. Choose a favorite story and either tell it or read it to your child. When you are near the end, stop and have your child finish the story by inventing a new ending. It can be funny or not. The same story can have several endings. Repeat this activity with another story.

287

If Toys Could Dance

Directions

Ask your child to collect a few of his or her favorite toys. Set them down with you and your child and talk about what would happen if each toy could move and dance. How would they dance? Let your child show you how each of her or his toys dances. Alternatively, ask your child, "If you were that toy, what kind of dance would you do?"

288

Cylinder City

289

Materials

1. Plywood or strong cardboard
2. Paper cylinders — all sizes
3. Paints and paint brushes
4. Scissors
5. Tape
6. Glue

Directions

Cut some of the cylinders across to increase the range of sizes and shapes of the cylinder collection. Dip one end of each cylinder in glue and set on the cardboard or plywood. Hold until the cylinder is stable. Your child should make all the decisions about where each cylinder should be placed. Allow all the cylinders to dry. If the cylinders are sufficiently stable they can be painted and decorated. Give your city a name, state, and zip code.

290

Snip Snap

Materials
1. 6-pack rings
2. Scissors

Directions

Plastic 6-pack rings often wind up in the ocean and can kill sea birds and fish when their heads get caught in the rings. When your child finds a 6-pack ring, show him or her how to use the scissors to snip the plastic into small sections. Put the sections in the garbage or in a plastic recycling bin.

Two Tone
Etched Cookies

Materials

1. Graham crackers
2. 2 oz. dark chocolate
3. Marshmallow topping
4. 1 Tbsp. butter
5. Double boiler
6. Knife, brush, skewer

291

Directions

Melt the chocolate and butter in the top of a double boiler until smooth. Spread the graham crackers with the marshmallow topping. Dip the brush into the chocolate and paint over the marshmallow. Refrigerate the crackers for about 30 minutes. Take the skewer (or a clean nail) and scratch the chocolate layer to expose the white layer beneath. Etch different designs on each cracker. Share and eat.

Winter
Tracks

Directions

If you are in an area which has snow in the winter, you can organize a winter tracking expedition. This is best done when the snow is still fresh. Look for imprints in the snow and try to ascertain which animal might have made them. If necessary, get a book on animal tracks to help you. Follow the tracks and see where they lead. You and your child can make your own tracks—walking, running, and jumping. Or put your feet in each other's tracks to see how it feels.

292

Lifesize Me in PJ's

Materials
1. Brown wrapping paper or plain newsprint
2. Felt marker
3. Scissors
4. Paints and thick paint brushes

Directions

Roll out paper and tape it down on the floor. Have your child lie down on the paper on his or her back or front pretending to be asleep. Trace around the outline of the child's body with a felt marker. When the child gets up, suggest that he or she paint on the outline as if they were going to bed. Draw and color pajamas, slippers, nightdress, and perhaps a favorite bedtime toy. When finished, cut out the outline and tape to the back of the bedroom door or above the bed.

294

Jump the River

Materials
1. Sandbox or beach
2. Stick

Directions

With the stick make a long straight line. Make another line about 6" away from the first line. The lines represent the banks of the river and the idea is to jump across the river without getting wet. Take turns to run and jump over the river. When it gets easy, draw the lines further apart. To make the jump more challenging place large and small objects in the river, such as toys, sticks, and make-believe boats. A winding river is interesting too.

Fun Sign Language

295

Directions

Involve your child in making up signals with the hands, arms, and fingers. Each signal should stand for a word or expression. Keep it simple and see how many your child can remember. This could become a game—a secret or private language between you and your child.

Rubbish Rubbings

Materials
1. Black, brown, or dark blue crayons
2. White drawing paper

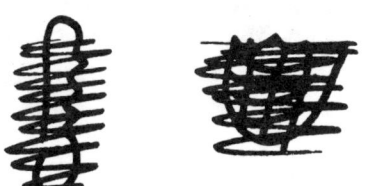

Directions
Look around inside and outside with your child to try to find some textured surfaces on which to make rubbings. Small objects such as coins are good to start with. Later try manhole covers, plaques, stucco, etc. Place the paper over the object and rub firmly back and forth with a crayon. An outline will soon appear. Rubbings can also be made of leaves, keys, woven baskets, and sidewalk cracks.

296

Only a Song

Directions

You and your child are going to play a game of songs. You will sing everything to her or him instead of talking. He or she has to sing back. The quality of your singing isn't of concern. The important thing is to sing everything. For example, sing, "How are you this morning?" and, "Are you ready for your breakfast?"

298 Flowering Names

Materials
1. Wildflower seeds
2. Stick
3. Garden plot

Directions

Prepare the soil of a section of the garden—about 4' x 3'. Remove stones, weeds, and other debris. Smooth over. Using the stick write your child's name in the soil making the groove 1" deep. Evenly sprinke the wildflower seeds in the lines. Instead of covering the seeds with soil, simply press them into the grooves with the hands or the edge of the stick. Even before the plants flower, your child will be able to discern his or her name as the seedlings appear. You could also make a flower picture of one of your child's drawings.

Act It Out

Materials

1. An adventure story

Directions

Read your child an exciting adventure story. When you have finished, plan to reenact it with suggestions from your child for props and scenes Use chairs, cushions, and other furniture to set the stage. Involve other members of the family if needed. Act out the story in front of an audience or just between yourselves.

299

Body Sculpting

Directions

Ask your child to pretend that he or she is a soft lump of playdough and that you are the sculptor. Gently move your child's body into different shapes and positions. Then try bending, turning, and lifting your child's body. Next it is your child's turn to be the sculptor. Stand, sit, or lie while he or she shapes your body. Offer no resistance and hold each new position still until your child moves it again.

300

Pinwheels

301

Materials
1. Strong construction paper or wallpaper
2. Long dressmaking pin
3. Penny
4. Pencil with eraser or thin dowel
5. Crayons or felt pens

Directions

Cut the paper into a square shape—6" x 4" would be suitable. If using plain paper, now is the time to apply decorations with crayons or felt pens. Draw in the diagonals, corner to corner. Trace around a penny in the center of the diagonal lines. Remove penny and then cut along the diagonals from each corner to the edge of the circle in the center. Fold (without creasing) each corner into the center and fasten together with the pin. Stick the pin firmly into the top of the dowel or the eraser of the pencil. Hold into the wind or attach to handlebars of bike.

302 My Family is Good

Directions

This day would be a nice day to sit down with your child and talk about the good qualities of your family. Take one family member at a time and bring up every good point you can think of. Encourage your child to contribute with positive comments and ideas. When you have discussed everyone, then talk about forgiveness and tolerance. Say how we should always look for the good in each person. Being aware of the goodness in our friends and family will help us forgive them when they disappoint us or let us down.

Edible Jewelry

Materials

1. Lifesavers candy
2. Cheerios or Fruit Loops
3. Popcorn
4. Miniature marshmallows
5. Dried fruits
6. Thread
6. Darning needle

Directions

Begin by threading the needle with yarn or thread. Now see if your child can make an interesting necklace or bracelet by threading a variety of foodstuffs together. When your child is finished, he or she can wear and eat the results.

303

Ocean Waves

Materials
1. Large plastic soda bottle (not glass)
2. Vegetable oil
3. Blue food coloring
4. Water

Directions
Rinse bottle and remove labels. Fill one bottle half-full with water and one a quarter full with oil. Add a few drops of food coloring. Tightly screw on the bottle cap. Have your child gently rock the bottle back and forth to create waves.

304

Bean Bag Buddies

305

Materials

1. Old mitten
2. Felt and fabric pieces
3. Glue (for attaching fabric)
4. Dried beans or rice

Directions

Decorate mitten with cutout shapes from felt and fabric pieces. Mitten can be made to look like an animal, person, or robot. Glue shapes on securely. Fill mitten with a handful of dried beans or rice. Have an adult stitch up the opening of the glove so that none of the beans or rice can escape. Beanbag buddy can be cuddled, tossed, or played with.

306 Houses of Cards

Materials
1. Playing cards
2. Flat surface

Directions

The object of this activity is to see how many cards your child can use in constructing a house or apartment building. Start with 10 cards and keep adding cards as the building gets bigger and higher. When the house ultimately collapses, count all the cards that were used. If playing with a partner, make separate houses or see what your combined efforts will produce.

Transportation Collage

Materials

1. Old magazines
2. Scissors
3. Glue or paste
4. Cardboard
5. Black felt pen

307

Directions

Sit with your child and go through old magazines looking for pictures of cars, boats, planes, and other means of travel. Also look for pictures which show people (especially children) inside these vehicles. Cut them out and have your child arrange them on the sheet of cardboard. Glue or paste them to form a collage. When the glue dries, label some of the pictures with a black felt pen. When a parent has to travel somewhere, use the collage to show how.

Body Beautiful

Materials
1. Large sheet of butcher or brown paper
2. Crayons or paints
3. Black felt marker
4. Scissors (optional)

Directions
Have your child lie down on the paper in any shape he or she wants. Trace around the body with a felt marker. Have your child take over and draw his or her own features and clothes on the outline. It can be what he or she is actually wearing or what he or she would like to be dressed in—a halloween costume, for instance. The outline can be cut out or left on the large sheet and then hung up.

308

Louder, Softer Please

309

Directions

Sing a familiar song, such as "Yankee Doodle." Start singing it loud and gradually sing more softly as if Yankee Doodle were riding off into the distance. Sing some more of the song, this time getting louder and louder as if he were riding towards you. This little exercise helps your child to understand the dynamics of sound and music. Both you and your child should sing songs together changing the volume to suit the words and meaning of the songs.

310 Life in the Desert

Materials
1. Tray
2. Potting soil mixed with sand
3. 6 small cacti
4. Small hand mirror
5. Plastic desert animals, such
   as camels, lizards, snakes

Directions

Spread the soil and sand mixture in the tray. Plant the cactus plants in the soil according to directions. Sprinkle very lightly with water. Place the mirror in the sand to create a mirage and put the animals among the cacti. To find out when to water your desert, check the weather conditions for Arizona in the newspaper. Whenever it rains in Arizona, that is when you water your cactus plants.

Mad Hatter

Materials

1. Cottage cheese carton
2. Crepe paper
3. 12" square sheet of cardboard - from a used box or carton
4. Old buttons

311

Directions

While a child wears a hat, he or she can become a different person. Cut a 12" circle out of the sheet of cardboard. Trace a circle within the cardboard circle using the cottage cheese carton. Make another circle an inch smaller inside the carton circle. Cut out the last (smallest) circle. Cut slashes up to the second circle and bend the cardboard upwards. Place the carton over these tabs and glue. Cover and decorate the resulting hat with crepe paper and buttons.

Swing, Slide, and Spin

Directions

In this activity, you and your child will imagine you are in a playground and there is nothing to play on. Instead, you will move the way the swing moves—running to and fro with your child. Or you can slide together as if you were on the slide, climbing up the stairs first. Finally, you can move in circles as if you were on the tire swing or the merry-go-round. There are also the teeter-totter and climbing bars to invent.

312

Cork Sculptures

313

Materials

1. Corks of different sizes and shapes
2. Glue
3. Toothpicks
4. Paints and paint brushes

Directions

Glue corks together to make familiar or imaginary shapes. Wait until glue dries. If your child wants to play with the sculptures in the bathtub, there is no need to paint them. Otherwise, apply colorful paints and wait until completely dry before using them.

314 Box Breakfast

Materials
1. Small boxes of cereal
2. Fresh fruit
3. Picnic foods and drinks
4. Boxes (e.g., shoeboxes)

Directions
This is an activity for a parent and child to do together on a weekend morning to surprise the rest of the family. Prepare boxed breakfasts for each member of the family the night before. The next morning, get up early and hide the breakfasts outside. Leave clues as to the whereabouts of their breakfasts at the table where they would normally sit. While they search for their boxes, set up a picnic table and enjoy a surprise picnic breakfast together.

Ice Cream Cone Cakes

Materials

1. Ice cream cones—flat bottomed
2. Cake mix
3. Frosting mix
4. Cake decorations
5. Muffin pan

Directions

Prepare the cake mix according to directions. Spoon the batter into the cones until they are 2/3 full. Place the cones in the muffin pan and bake according to the package directions. When the cakes are cool, frost and decorate them.

Driftwood Sea Garden

Materials

1. Interesting piece of driftwood
2. Dried seaweed
3. Assorted sea shells
4. Glue

Directions

Rinse and dry off driftwood. Set it on a flat surface. Rinse shells and shake the sand out of the seaweed. When all these materials are dry, glue them securely on the driftwood to make an under water sea garden. When finished, an adult can spray the garden with clear varnish or acrylic to make it appear shiny.

316

Fabric Weaving

Materials

1. Large fabric scraps or pieces
2. Scissors

Directions

Before child starts weaving, cut a large square out of fabric—canvas or a heavyweight fabric is best for this square "frame." Leave an inch around the outside edge and then cut lines about 3" apart inside the square all going in one direction. Take the remaining fabric and cut narrow strips out of it. Give these strips to your child and show him or her how to weave them in and out of the square. After the square is completely woven, stitch around the edge with sewing machine to prevent unraveling. Use as a doll's blanket or place mat.

318

Who Am I?

Directions

Your child is going to ask questions which require a YES or NO answer in order to find out who or what you are thinking of. Your job is to choose a person, place, or thing within your child's environment or knowledge range and keep it secret until your child has guessed correctly. He or she asks questions such as, is it real? Is it in my bedroom? Can I eat it?

Long Distance Sounds

Materials
1. 2 paper cups
2. Long piece of string

Directions

This is how to make a simple long distance telephone. Pierce a small hole in the bottom of each paper cup. Thread the string through each hole and tie a knot so that the cups are connected. Now each of you take a cup and stand apart from each other, keeping the string taut. One talks into the cup while the other puts the cup to his or her ear. If the words are not easy to understand, just make different sounds.

Salt Pictures

Materials

1. Salt
2. Dry tempera paints—in powder form
3. Drawing paper
4. Glue
5. Baby food jars

Directions

Mix the salt with the paint powder in a baby food jar, a separate jar for each color. Have your child either brush or dribble the glue to make patterns on the drawing paper. She or he may wish to spread the glue around more with the fingers. Now sprinkle the salt mixture over the paper using one or more colors. Wait until the glue dries and then tip off the excess colored salt. Make several pictures and hang the collection in the hallway.

320

Nursery Rhyme Rhythms

321

Materials

1. A homemade drum or an empty oatmeal box
2. Other hand held musical toys

humpy Dumpty

Directions

While chanting or singing a nursery rhyme, have your child tap it out on the drum or oatmeal box. This musical activity can be made more challenging and interesting by adding other instruments as accents. The adult taps out the basic rhythm while the child accents with bells, spoons, or shakers.

322

Carrot Baskets

Materials

1. A really fat carrot
2. 3 paper clips
3. Toothpicks
4. Heavy thread or string

Directions

Remove the leaves from the carrot. Cut a 3" piece from the top of the carrot and scoop out some of the insides to make a bowl-shape. Open up the paper clips and push the straight end into the carrot about 1/2" from the top of the bowl. Cut thread into three 12" lengths and tie each one to a paper clip. Knot them together at the other end. Stick some shortened toothpicks into the carrot. Fill the carrot's bowl with water and hang in a sunny place, such as in front of the kitchen window. Soon the carrot's leaves will grow back and form a green basket.

Pirates and
Gypsies

Materials
1. Bandanas
2. Black construction paper
3. Rubber bands or elastic
4. White or silver paper
5. Scissors
6. Necklaces or strings of beads

323

Directions

In order to play pirates and gypsies, it is necessary to prepare the costumes — scarves, eye-patches, necklaces, and earrings. To make the eye-patches, cut a circle out of the black paper and thread rubber bands through the sides so that they stretch around your child's head. Cut a circle out of white or silver paper and cut out the inside, leaving a width of 1/2 an inch. Slash the ring and hook it around or onto your child's ear. Lastly, tie the bandana around her or his head and drape the necklaces.

Dance Notation

Directions

Find some very different types of music to play. Provide your child with paper and crayons. Explain that after she or he has danced each selection of the music, you want your child to draw the dance on the paper. Encourage your child to dance creatively and draw boldly and expressively.

324

Tugboat

325

Materials

1. A quart milk carton
2. Empty small seasoning boxes
3. Tube from toilet paper roll
4. Glue

Directions

Cut milk carton in half lengthwise to make the boat bottom (hull). Glue two of the small seasoning boxes together to make the cabin. Glue the toilet paper roll to the back of the cabin to make the smokestack. Finally, glue the cabin and smokestack onto the bottom of the boat. See if it will float in the bathtub.

326

Paper Press

Materials
1. Newspaper
2. Blender
3. 12 x 8 inch piece of screening
4. 13 x 9 inch tray
5. Small wooden board

Directions

Make your own paper. Tear 3 pages of a newspaper into small pieces. Drop pieces into a blender and add 5 cups of water. Blend until paper is turned into pulp. Pour the pulp onto the screen in the tray to drain, spreading pulp evenly. Lift out the screen and place inside several sheets of dry newspaper. Flip over the newspaper so the screen is on top of the pulp. Press out the excess water with the board. Open the newspaper and remove the screen. Leave the newspaper and let the pulp dry. When dry, carefully peel the new paper off the newspaper. It can now be used to write or draw on.

Cookie Paint

Materials

1. 3 egg yolks
2. 1 teaspoon water
3. 1 teaspoon corn syrup
4. Food coloring
5. 3 paper cups
6. Paint brushes

327

Directions

Before preparing paint, roll out some plain cookie dough and have your child cut out cookie shapes and set them on a baking tray. Beat the egg yolks with the water and corn syrup. Divide into 3 paper cups. Add a different food color to each cup. Go ahead and bake the cookies. 3 minutes before they are done, remove from oven and let your child paint them. Return tray to oven and finish cooking. Cool before eating.

Field and Forest Sounds

Materials
Blanket

Directions
Take your child to an open field or to a forest clearing.
Spread the blanket and lie down. Listen quietly to
nature's sounds. Raise a hand when an interesting sound is
heard. Talk about the sound and ask where it came from.
Who made it? Was it an animal or a bird or an insect?
The wind makes interesting sounds too. Listen to it move
through the leaves, the grass, or the trees. Discuss why
sounds are a part of our natural environment.

328

Surprise Nut Tree

329

Materials
1. Walnut shells
2. Ribbon
3. Small tree branch
4. Tiny surprises to put into walnut shells
5. Used plastic pot with soil in it

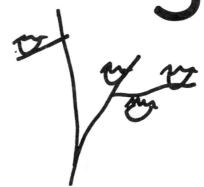

Directions
Fill the walnut shells with tiny surprises, such as M&M's, nuts, raisins, etc. Glue or tape the shells together and tie a length of ribbon around each one. Push the branch into the soil in the pot so that it is secure. Tie the shells to the branch by the ribbons so they hang free. Your child can snip the ribbon with scissors and open the shells to find what's inside.

330

Air Bowling

Materials
1. Ball
2. Net to hold ball
3. 9 empty quart milk cartons
4. Rope

Directions

Place ball in the net and, using rope, suspend the ball from the branch of a tree. The ball should nearly touch the ground. Arrange the cartons in a diamond shape under the ball and to one side. The object of the game is to strike the ball and see how many cartons can be knocked down. If playing with a friend, have 3 strikes each and see who can knock over the most.

My Own Scales

Materials

1. Wire coat hanger
2. 2 strong paper plates
3. 4 pieces of string, 30"
   long

Directions

Make 4 small holes in the edges of each paper plate. Using 2 lengths of string per plate, thread them through the holes to make a cross on the back of the plates. Hang plates from each corner of the hanger. Hang the coat hanger from a door knob. Find some small stones or marbles and place on one of the plates. Now find other things that will balance the other plate. Try other balances, e.g., Is a cookie heavier than some grapes?

331

Contour Line Art

Materials
1. Drawing paper
2. Black felt pen
3. Crayons

Directions

Have your child make a large closed shape, such as a heart, box, ball, or triangle with the black felt pen. Starting on the inside near the shape's edge, repeat the outline. Continue redrawing it, getting it smaller and smaller until it cannot be repeated. Now, color in each contour with different colored crayons. Don't worry if your child goes over the lines. This activity can go in reverse, i.e., start with a small shape and draw several outlines on the outside.

332

Milk Carton Guitar

333

Materials

1. Milk carton—any size
2. Yardstick
3. Fishing line or nylon thread
4. 6 screw eyes

Directions

Stand carton upright and cut vertical slots on either side about 1" from the top, big enough for the yardstick to go through. Insert the yardstick. Cut notches in the top of the carton for the strings—about 3 or 4. Put the same number of screw eyes in each end of the yardstick and screw in until they are secure. Now, tie the string to the screw eyes at one end, run them over the top of the carton and tie them to the screw eyes at the other end. Tighten so that the strings produce a guitar-like sound. To play, either strum or pluck.

334

Elf Garden

Materials
1. Foil pie plate
2. Soil
3. Moss
4. Hand mirror
5. Tiny plants, ferns, or seedlings

Directions

Pack some soil into the pie plate. Proceed to make a simple garden of small proportions. Use the moss to give contours. Place the mirror on the soil to make a pond. Insert the plants around the mirror and between the clumps of moss. Keep moist by sprinkling lightly with water. Keep out of direct sunlight. Imagine the elves that might live there.

Up the Hill

335

Directions

Take your child to a grassy slope. Explore the different ways he or she can climb the slope and then come down again. Try to do it the way animals would (e.g., birds, grasshoppers, elephants, worms, and monkeys). Go up like one animal and come down like another. Or try going up fast and coming down slowly. Think of other imaginative ways you and your child can enjoy the incline.

Chiffon Dancing

Directions

Provide yourself and your child with chiffon scarves. Throw them into the air and watch them float down to the ground. After each scarf has settled, imitate the scarf movements in the air and down to the ground with your own movements. Try this several times. Drape the scarf over your head or shoulders and dance. Think of other ways that you and your child can dance with the scarves expressing the lightness of the fabric.

336

Plaster Box Etchings

337

Materials

1. Plaster of paris
2. Oil or Vaseline
3. Aluminum pan
4. Nails
5. Paints and paint brushes
6. Damp cloth or sandpaper

Directions

Mix plaster of paris according to directions and pour into pan. Let it set until quite dry and firm. Turn out onto a paper-covered flat surface. Use nails and other sharp objects to scratch or carve a design or picture. Lightly brush paint over the etched surface and wait until it dries. Using a damp cloth or sandpaper, remove the surface paint until only the colored etching is exposed. Prop up the finished etching on a shelf or mantlepiece for everyone to see.

338

The Tree of Life

Materials
1. A large tree with many branches

Directions

Children see trees almost every day. Trees can be used to remind children of the connectedness of all life, and of human beings in particular. Have your child look at each branch and see where it comes from and where it leads to. Imagine one little twig is your family. The branch would be your neighborhood, and a larger branch, your town. All the branches connect to form your country and the whole tree represents all the countries in the world. Notice how we all have the same trunk and roots. Notice how we all need each other in order to make a beautiful and healthy tree.

Collage Melt

Materials

1. Sliced cold cuts
2. Cheese slices
3. Bread
4. Tomato
5. Scissors and knife
6. Broiler

339

Directions

Butter the slices of bread and place face down on a cookie sheet. Use scissors to cut the meat and cheese into small shapes. Slice tomato into small pieces. Have your child decorate each bread slice making colorful collages. Put the cookie tray under the broiler for a few minutes until the cheese melts and the shapes all run together. Cool and eat.

Nature Book

Materials
1. Notepad
2. Pencil or crayon
3. Glue stick
4. Paper bag

Directions
Take your child on a nature walk with a paper bag, notepad, pencil, and glue stick. Stop when you see something the child finds interesting. If it is small enough, glue it onto the notepaper. Write down what your child notices about it — color, shape, texture, smell, etc. Continue to collect things and write about them on separate sheets of paper. When you get home, staple the pages together into a nature book.

340

Easy Stained Glass

341

Materials

1. White glue
2. Flat dish or pan
3. Pipe cleaners
4. Food colors
5. Piece of plastic foam

Directions

Protect the work surface with newspaper. Dilute the white glue with water (half and half), add some food color and pour into flat dish or pan. Take the pipe cleaners and shape the ends into circles, oblongs, or whatever shape desired. The shapes must be closed. Dip the shapes into the glue and hold over the pan until the glue stops dripping. Stick the pipe cleaner into the foam to dry. Use smaller pans with several colors for more variety. Colored "glass" shapes can be used for decorations or can be strung together and hung in front of a window.

342

Pick-up Sticks

Materials
1. Wooden meat skewers
2. Paints
3. Paint brushes
4. Empty baby food jars

Directions
Put paints into baby food jars - a different color per jar. Dip each end of a meat skewer into the same color paint. Dry one end before putting in the other end. Dip ONE skewer into some black paint. To play the game, hold all the skewers in both hands upright. Let the skewers fall. The object of the game is to remove the skewers from the pile without disturbing any other skewer. The black one can be used to flick or poke. Take turns after an error is made.

What Fits In This Jar?

Materials

1. Large sheet of paper
2. Pencil or black pen

343

Directions

Draw the outlines of a variety of different shaped jars—tall and thin, short and round, large and rectangular. Ask your child to think of things that would fit inside each jar. Help him or her think of things that are not normally found in jars and see if they would fit. Either draw them from memory or ask your child to bring some items to you and test them out on the jar drawings. Some of them might fit inside, but may not be able to pass down the opening.

Picture Paperweight

Materials
1. A smooth rock
2. Child's photo
3. Waxed paper
4. Tempera paint
5. Liquid glue
6. Paint brush

Directions
Mix 1/4 cup of tempera paint with 1/4 cup of glue. Clean and dry rock and place it on waxed paper. Have your child paint the rock with the glue mixture. While still wet, carefully press the photo onto the rock. Let it dry completely before using as a paperweight.

344

Paint a Song

345

Materials

1. Butcher paper
2. Crayons, markers, or paints
3. Taped or recorded music

Directions

Sit on the floor with your child and spread a large piece of the butcher paper between you. Have the crayons, markers, and paints handy and ready to use. Put on some music and close your eyes for a minute or so to get the "feel" of the sound and rhythm. Open your eyes and draw the music as you hear it. The drawings should reflect the rhythm, dynamics, tempo, and mood of the music rather than represent a person, place, or thing.

346  Tiny Basket Planter

Materials
1. Plastic berry container
2. Ribbons
3. Potting soil
4. Seeds
5. Foil

Directions
Weave ribbons in and out of basket spaces until all spaces are filled. Line basket with some foil. Fill with potting soil and moisten. Sprinkle seeds on top of soil and press down. Cover basket with plastic until seeds germinate. Water often with a fine spray. Basket can be hung or placed on a window ledge.

Talking Heads

Materials

1. Paper plate
2. Felt markers or crayons
3. Strips of strong paper
4. Tape or stapler
5. Ruler or flat stick

347

Directions

Draw a face on the underside of the paper plate. Attach the ruler or stick behind the chin. In place of the mouth, cut out two vertical slits 2" apart to cover your child's lips. On the strip of paper draw several mouth expressions, such as a smile, a pout, an angry expression, and a sad one. Now thread the strip through the slits. Hold the mask in front of the face. Pull the paper slowly through the slits and have your child invent a monologue.

Spaghetti Dance

Directions

Lie down on the floor with your child very stiff and straight. Imagine you are uncooked spaghetti and roll over and over. Now imagine you are being put into hot water to cook. Feel your bodies getting softer and softer. When the water boils, make your bodies swirl and twist just as spaghetti would. Finally, imagine you have been drained and tossed with butter or sauce. What movements would result?

348

Picture Frames

349

Materials
1. Cardboard from a carton
2. Fabric remnants
3. Glue or paste
4. Thumbtacks

Directions
Remove the side of a cardboard carton. Cut the fabric several inches larger than the size of the cardboard. Miter the corners to fit. Attach the fabric to the cardboard with glue, stretching it to make a smooth surface. Let the glue dry before mounting the child's artwork with thumbtacks. For a permanent frame, glue the artwork directly onto the fabric.

350

Zoo Project

Directions

Your child can help save and protect endangered animals. Call the local children's zoo or nature reserve. Ask if it has an 'animal adoption' program. If so, let your child choose an animal, preferably an endangered species, and see how much he or she can learn about it. Perhaps there will be some things he or she can do for the animal or ways your child can help the zoo save more animals from extinction.

Licorice Necklace

Materials

1. Shoestring licorice
2. Marshmallows
3. Cookies with holes
4. Pretzels

Directions

Use the licorice as the necklace string. Tie more than one length together to make a longer necklace. Thread the licorice through the marshmallows, cookies, pretzels, and any other food that can be penetrated. Tie the finished necklace around your child's neck and he or she can eat parts of it whenever hungry. This is a good birthday party activity.

351

Habitat Happenings

Directions

Take a walk through your neighborhood or just go around the block. Notice and discuss all the things that make it a living neighborhood—the people, gardens, plants, lawns, animals, trees, insects, and birds. Explain that all the living things make it a habitat and that town habitats are often different from country habitats. But everywhere, animals and plants must live together in harmony in order to survive.

352

Clothespin Hang-ups

Materials

1. Poster board
2. Spring-type wooden clothespins
3. Paints and paint brushes
4. Glue
5. Yarn
6. Hole punch

Directions

Cover work area with newspapers. Mix paints and pour into muffin pans or paper cups. Punch holes in upper corners of poster board. Paint over poster board until all or most of it is covered. While the poster board is drying, paint the clothespins too. When the clothespins are dry, glue them onto the poster board. Let glue dry and then thread some of the yarn through the holes in the clothespins which are next to each other. Tie yarn leaving a loop between clothespins. Now your child has a bulletin board on which to hang things and clip papers. Attach the poster board to a wall via the punched holes.

354

Indoor Baseball

Materials

1. Old newspaper
2. Masking tape

Directions

Crunch some newspaper into a big ball. Start with a small ball shape and pack newspaper sheets around it. Apply masking tape to hold the ball's shape. Roll up more newspaper to form a bat shape. Find a place inside or outside the house where your child has room to run. Give your child the bat and throw the ball to him or her. When contact is made, your child must run to a "base" before you retrieve the ball and tag him or her. Be prepared to repair or replace the bats often!

Fill in the Rainbow

Materials

1. Colorful fabric
2. Old magazines
3. Scissors
4. Pencils
5. Paper—large sheet
6. Glue

355

Directions

Draw the outline of a rainbow onto the paper. Show your child which color goes in which area of the rainbow by pasting on a scrap of fabric or a piece of colored paper. Explain to your child to only glue on the same color in each separate ring. Go through the fabric and magazines to find the different colors. This project could take several sessions and might be a good one for other members of the family to help with.

Karate String Art

Materials
1. White paper
2. Tempera paints
3. Baby food jars
4. Strong string

Directions
Mix the paints and pour into jars. Cut the string into various lengths—6", 9", 12", and 18". Tape paper down on a flat surface. Dip a length of string into paint and either drag or 'karate chop' it onto the paper. Repeat with a different color. Cover the paper with color and line. When dry, the artwork can be used as a gift wrap or mounted and hung on a wall.

356

Bottle Top Castanets

357

Materials

1. Cardboard
2. 4 bottle caps

Directions

Cut cardboard into two 8" strips. Fold each strip in half and glue a bottle cap to each end on the inside. To use the castanets, the child holds a folded cardboard strip in each hand with the bottle caps facing. The bottle caps will click together when the hands are opened and closed.

358

Leaf Log

Materials
1. Paper bag
2. Heavy book
3. Scotch tape
4. Blank page notebook

Directions

On a fine day, go walking with your child and collect leaves. Fresh leaves are best. Put them in the paper bag. When you get home, press the leaves between absorbent paper (coffee filters are best) in a heavy book. Leave for a day or two. Remove the pressed leaves from the book and attach them to the blank pages of the notebook with Scotch tape. Try to identify each leaf and then write its name on the page. Build the leaf log by taking walks to different places or by collecting leaves seasonally.

Grandma and Grandpa

Materials

1. Large sheet of white paper
2. Pencil or black pen
3. Photos of grandparents

Directions

Have your child recount a story about his or her grandparent(s). It could be something your child has actually experienced or something he or she would like to. Write down what your child tells you on the paper. When you have finished with the story, illustrate it with drawings and photos. Fold it neatly and then send it to the lucky grandparent(s).

359

Growing and Shrinking

Directions

Stand where you have lots of room. Imagine you and your child are each in a giant bubble. Reach out and try to touch the walls of the bubble. Imagine the bubble begins to get smaller and smaller until you can hold it in your hand. Squeeze it up and hold it tightly in your hand. Now let it go and feel it expand all around you again. As the bubble gets bigger you and your child grow bigger too. Finish by putting the tight space into a drawer to use again later.

360

Tennis Ball Puppet

361

Materials
1. Tennis ball
2. Cloth napkin or men's handkerchief
3. Paints, crayons, or markers
4. Thumbtacks (optional)

Directions
Cut a hole in the base of the tennis ball big enough for the child's finger. Make the tennis ball into a face with paints, crayons, and markers. Use thumbtacks for eyes. Glue on yarn or colored paper for hair. Place the napkin over the child's hand and have him insert his or her index finger into the tennis ball base. The child's thumb and middle finger will be the puppet's arms. Attach the napkin to the "arm" fingers with a loose rubber band. Now the puppet is ready for action.

362

Helping Others

Directions

Today you are going to talk to your child about caring for others. Think of ways your child can help the members of the family. Think also of ways your child can help others. Here are some suggestions—picking up your brother or sister's toys for them, saying hello to everyone, smiling, helping in the yard, etc. When your child does these things, do not forget to thank them or praise them so as to reinforce the habit of helping others.

Outer Space Cookies

Materials

1. Chilled cookie dough
2. Anise seeds
3. Cutting tools and objects

Directions

On a floured board or table, roll out the cookie dough. Have your child cut out and shape cookies that might have come from outer space. Make impressions on the cookie shapes with Legos®, forks, fingers, and other textured objects. Sprinkle the anise seeds on the greased cookie tray. Place the cookies carefully on the tray and bake for 15 minutes at 350 degrees F.

363

My Walking Stick

Materials
1. Thick, sturdy stick
2. House or furniture paint
3. Paint thinner (optional)
4. Paint brush
5. Sandpaper

Directions
Go on a hike with your child and find a child-size walking stick. Take it home and wash it. Let it dry completely and sand it down with sandpaper until smooth to the touch. Paint the stick with bright colors. Let the paint dry. Now everytime you and your child go walking, the painted walking stick can go along too. Sticks are great for turning over rocks, poking the earth, and pointing at things.

364

Snowman Alive

365

Materials

1. Paper grocery bag
2. Cotton balls (white)
3. White tissue paper
4. Glue
5. White styrofoam

Directions

Place bag over child's head and mark eyes and armholes. Remove bag and cut out holes for eyes and arms. Put bag over the back of a chair so that it can be walked around. Dip cotton balls into saucer of glue and attach to the paper bag. Scrunch up small pieces of the tissue paper and do likewise. Dip styrofoam pieces into glue and add them too. Continue until the bag is totally covered. Mound extra balls of tissue onto the top of the bag to give a rounded look. Wait until the glue dries before the child wears the snowman costume and acts out a snowman story.

Index

Foods and Cooking

Games

The authors and publisher wish to thank the special group of five to seven year olds from the San Francisco Bay Area who provided all the wonderful illustrations for our book.

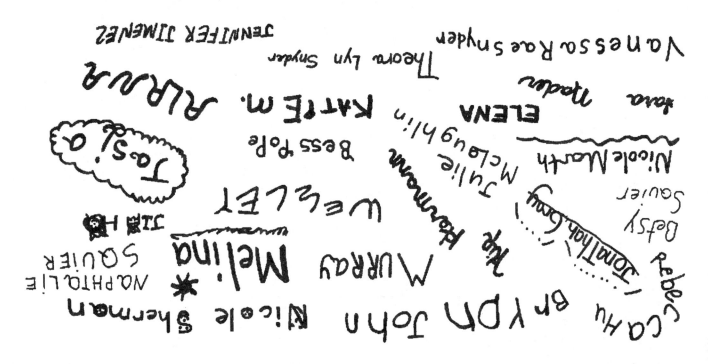

About the Authors

Sheila Ellison has a B.A. degree in psychology from the University of Southern California, and is the creator and author of the very popular and successful "365" series of parenting books, including *365 Foods Kids Love to Eat* and *365 Afterschool Activities*. These books have grown out of Sheila's lifelong involvement with children, her many volunteer efforts on their behalf, and her founding of community youth groups and mentoring programs. The mother of four children, she has recently completed national media tours presenting her ideas on successful parenting along with new products that make life with children easier. She is currently writing her next work.

Dr. Judith Gray is internationally known as an author, teacher, leader in dance research, and speaker on future trends in education and dance. A former Executive Director of the Girl's Club of Tucson, Dr. Gray has been an educator at both the high school and university level. A mother of four, she is currently helping to develop a state-of-the-art high school in the Everett School District, Washington, and is on the Antioch University teaching faculty. Dr. Gray is also the co-author of *365 Foods Kids Love to Eat*.

Hungry For More Childcare Tips?
Don't Miss
365 Foods Kids Love To Eat
Nutritious and Kid-tested
by Sheila Ellison and Judith Gray

365 Foods Kids Love To Eat is the cookbook parents have been waiting for! This cookbook contains carefully chosen, kitchen-tested recipes that appeal to the whole family, especially those kids with finicky appetites.

"With its emphasis on variety, health, and simplicity, *365 Foods* is a boon to busy parents and hungry kids alike."
—*Parenting Magazine*

Written by the authors of *365 Days of Creative Play*, **365 Foods Kids Love To Eat** is a practical, easy-to-follow cookbook designed with kid's palates in mind.

396 pages, ISBN: 1-57071-030-9, $12.95

To order this book or any other of our many publications, please contact your local bookseller, gift store, or call Sourcebooks at (708) 961-3900. Thank you for your interest!